MASS SHOOTINGS

Six Steps to Survival

John Matthews

Mass Shootings

Acknowledgment:

I would like to acknowledge the following group of dedicated individuals who have contributed their subject matter expertise to develop this project:

- Peggy van Wunnik, editing, design and formatting
- Boyang Zhang, research and preliminary design
- Joseph and Michael Matthews, simulation actors for photography

Mass Shootings: Six Steps to Survival

© Copyright 2013 John Matthews. All rights reserved.
CSI Publishing, Dallas, Texas.

ISBN 978-0-9888556-2-5

All rights reserved. Except as permitted under U. S. Copyright Act, no part of this publication may be reproduced in any form or by any means, or stored in a data retrieval system, without prior written approval of the author. This book is intended to provide accurate and authoritative information with respect to the subject matter covered. The information contained in the first section has been compiled primarily from news sources found online. Every effort has been made to reconcile any discrepancies in order to present the most accurate information possible. It is sold with the understanding that neither the publisher nor author is engaged in rendering legal aid or advice regarding the subject matter covered. If legal aid or other advice is desired, the services of a competent professional should be sought.

INTRODUCTION

We have all seen the shocking and heart-wrenching news accounts from places we might have never before heard of but which are are now forever burned into our American collective consciousness: *Littleton, Blacksburg, Tucson, Aurora*, and now *Newtown*. Mention Columbine or the "Batman" shooting, Virginia Tech, or the Congresswoman Gabrielle Giffords attack, and immediately our minds flash to news footage of carnage and chaos as we mentally replay the images of so many innocent victims. Perhaps the most mind-numbing of all was the tragedy in Newtown, Connecticut, in December 2012, where 20 elementary-school-aged children and six of their teachers lost their lives, and so many families were forever changed.

When news accounts of these attacks first hit our airwaves, our first question is usually WHY? Why did such a terrible event have to occur? Why would someone randomly take the lives of innocent people? Why? Why? Why?

Throughout the country, in offices, restaurants and homes, we stay glued to our favorite source of news and information. Whether from radio or television, from news reports viewed on our computer screens, from constant streams of Facebook posts or by Twitter updates, we seek answers. As details of the event begin to emerge, and pieces of the puzzle begin to fit together, eventually the majority of our questions regarding the attack are answered. We usually discover in fairly short time the *who, what, where, when* and *how*—sometimes even the *why* or the motive for the attack—but for many of us, one question always lurks in the back of our consciousness: **What would I do if I were ever involved in a mass shooting?** As we ask that question, as we run through various scenarios in our minds, we soon discover that we have questions we can't answer:

Mass Shootings

How would I respond to a heavily-armed gunman who is determined to kill as many people as possible? What would I do if I were caught in the wrong place at the wrong time: in a crowded movie theater, at a popular concert, out celebrating at a city festival, or simply eating lunch with my child at school?

What do I do? Do I have the knowledge and skills necessary to survive an attack? How do I save myself and help others?

All of these questions and more are answered in *Mass Shootings: Six Steps to Survival*, a book written specifically to give everyone the information and tools necessary to survive a mass shooting or active shooter assault.

Examining nearly 60 mass shootings that have occurred in the United States since 1980, this book focuses on the actions taken and the decisions made by those who survived these horrific attacks, as well as lessons learned from those who did not survive. Armed with this new information, the old axiom "fight or flight" is dispelled—or at least modified—with regard to this new breed of killer. Fight by yourself, and you are almost assuredly going to join the ranks of the victims, if not the overall body count; attempt to flee and present a target for the killer or draw his attention, and the chances are you will not make it out alive.

Designed as a compendium of lessons learned, this book is comprised of vital information gleaned from survivors who have successfully endured some of the most tragic and violent incidents in U.S. history. Neither condemning nor condoning such actions, but simply presenting and analyzing the data has allowed this author to glean both unique observations of strategies and tactics employed, and to develop a teachable model to use to improve one's chances of successfully surviving a mass shooting.

Mass Shootings

So what are your chances of being involved in a mass shooting? It really depends on how one defines this phenomenon. In this book we use the Federal Bureau of Investigation (FBI) definition of mass shooting, which is "four or more killed in a single event." Using that definition, a *USA Today* analysis of 146 mass shootings indicated that more than 900 people died in mass shootings during the past seven years.[1]

If one utilizes the statistics provided by the Brady Campaign to Prevent Gun Violence, the numbers increase even more dramatically. Based on their definition (three or more people killed/injured in a single incident), between the Columbine shooting in April 1999 and September of 2012, nearly 200 people were shot to death in mass killings. In the first nine months of September 2012, there were 80 deaths resulting from mass murders. These numbers do not include those who were injured. The Brady Campaign reports that by their definition, *there are an average of 20 mass shootings per year in the United States.*[2]

Mass Shootings: Six Steps to Survival presents an easy-to-understand and easy-to-remember model for every citizen of nearly any age. Armed with this vital information, citizens will be able to learn from the actual experiences of mass shooting survivors and understand both successful and unsuccessful tactics which were utilized by these individuals in past incidents. Beginning with the basics of escape and how to properly exit a public facility, through the need to conceal oneself from the offender, and finally to the last-resort effort of engagement, the average citizen will learn specific techniques to utilize in a mass shooting or violent incident.

Mass Shootings: Six Steps to Survival provides readers with the potentially life-saving information and techniques they will need in order to have a fighting chance in the most horrifying of mass shooting situations.

Mass Shootings

METHODOLOGY

The case analyses which follow examine a list of 58 mass shooting incidents from 1980 to the present. This book does not purport to represent the entire text of each individual survivor's story, but simply recounts actions or tactics taken which may identify common successful techniques for survival. For the purposes of this book, a mass shooting is considered an attack by one or more individuals where at least four people were killed.

For each shooting incident, the primary background information is shown in the following format:

Synopsis	*General overview of the events*
Type of Establishment	*Primary place where main incident occurred*
Environment	*Indoors, outdoors or both*
Motive	*Reason for the attack, if established*
Number killed	*Number killed during a single or consecutive attacks by perpetrator; does not include suicide of killer*
Number killed and injured	*Number killed and injured during a single or consecutive attacks by perpetrator; does not include suicide of killer*
Date of murders	*Date*
Weapons	*Type of weapon(s) used*
Location	*City and state*
Shooter status	*Final disposition of the offender*

Mass Shootings

In 2010, the U.S. Department of Homeland Security produced a document called <u>Active Shooter Response</u> and introduced its simple three-step model of *Run, Hide and Fight*. In this book those elements are used to categorize various actions taken by individuals during mass shootings. When actions were taken outside of the DHS model, an "*Other*" category was added to explain what transpired, indicating how it helped or hurt the individuals involved.

It is this author's hope that this book will illustrate how the *Run/Hide/Fight* model can be expanded upon to include additional life-saving information which may help individuals survive a deadly attack.

Case Studies - 1980s

Case #1 - First Baptist Church

Synopsis	Alvin Lee King, 45, opened fire with a rifle during a worship service at the First Baptist Church of Daingerfield, killing 5.
Type of Establishment	Church
Environment	Indoors
Motive	Revenge/anger
Number killed	5
Number killed and injured	15
Date of murders	June 22, 1980
Weapons	M1 carbine with bayonet; AR-15 rifle with bayonet; .22 caliber handgun; .38 caliber handgun
Location	Daingerfield, Texas
Shooter status	Attempted suicide before being arrested. Committed suicide in prison.

Overview

Alvin Lee King had allegedly sexually molested his daughter, and was scheduled to be tried for the crime on June 23, 1980. He attempted without success to find someone in the congregation of the First Baptist Church of Daingerfield to testify as a character witness on his behalf.

On the morning of June 22, King bound his wife to a kitchen chair, then dressed in combat gear and armed himself with four guns.

He drove to the church and burst into the sanctuary, where the congregation was singing the offertory hymn. Shouting "This is war," King opened fire with the AR-15 rifle. In less than a minute, five people were killed and 10 were wounded.[3]

King then went across the street to a fire station and shot himself in the head. He survived the injury and was charged with murder.

Run/Hide/FIGHT
Witnesses went after shooter

When Red McDaniel saw that his wife had been shot, he turned toward the shooter and charged him, placing him in a bear hug. He drove King out of the church even while taking shots to the chest. McDaniel died outside the church. Kenneth Lee Truitt also went after the shooter. A witness said that when he got to the door he leaped into the air toward King, who was just outside the door. King shot him.[4]

Case #2 – Bob Moore's Welding & Machine Shop

Synopsis	Carl Robert Brown, 51, opened fire inside a welding shop and was later shot dead by two witnesses as he fled the scene.
Type of Establishment	Business/workplace
Environment	Indoors
Motive	Argument/retaliation
Number killed	8
Number killed and injured	11
Date of murders	August 20, 1982
Weapon	Shotgun
Location	Miami, Florida
Shooter status	Fatally shot and run down by two witnesses, when cycling away from the crime scene

Overview

On August 20, 1982, Navy veteran and teacher Carl Robert Brown, on psychiatric leave from his job,[5] rode his bicycle to a Miami welding and machine shop, entered through a side door, and began shooting. He was apparently angry at the $20 repair bill for work on his lawnmower engine. Brown walked through the building, methodically shooting everyone, most of the time at close range and sometimes twice, leaving three victims in the office and others in the work area and the driveway in front of the shop.[6]

Running out of ammunition, Brown stepped out of the store, reloaded and entered the shop again, to shoot twice more.

Brown then got back on his bicycle and pedaled away. At the shop, six of the 11 employees present were dead, and two more were dying.

RUN/Hide/Fight

Three of the injured managed to escape and jump into the car of a passing motorist, who brought them to a gas station a mile away and called for help.[7]

Run/Hide/Fight/OTHER
Witnesses went after shooter

Mark Kram heard the gunshots from his nearby shop, and stepped out to see what was happening. Ernest Hammett, who worked across the street, ran toward him, crying: "A bunch of people just got killed at Bob's!" Kram grabbed two guns from his office, one for himself, one for Hammett. He got behind the wheel of his car and Hammett got in the back seat. Six blocks away, he saw Brown on his bicycle.

As Kram pulled up alongside the teacher, Brown made a shoulder motion as if he were about to bring his shotgun around and open fire. Hammett, from the back seat, pointed the revolver out the driver's window. Kram said he grabbed the gun to steady Hammett's hand and fired what they meant to be a warning shot.

The bullet pierced Brown's back and severed his aorta, but Brown kept going on the bike, and "that's why I swerved my car into him," Kram said. Brown went flying into a concrete utility pole. The medical examiner's report revealed that the gunshot killed Brown.[8]

Case #3 - Ianni's Nightclub

Synopsis	Abdelkrim Belachheb, 39, opened fire at a nightclub after a woman rejected his advances. He was later arrested.
Type of Establishment	Nightclub
Environment	Indoors
Motive	Retaliation for rejection
Number killed	6
Number killed and injured	7
Date of murders	June 29, 1984
Weapons	9mm automatic pistol
Location	Dallas, Texas
Shooter status	Sentenced to six consecutive life terms in prison on November 15, 1984

Overview

After a brief argument with his dance partner Marcelle Ford at Ianni's, an upscale night club, unemployed waiter Abdelkrim Belachneb, a Moroccan national allowed entry into this country in spite of a violent record in Europe,[9] came back into the club with a 9mm automatic pistol which he shot at Ford and four others sitting at the bar.

Belachheb went outside to reload, then came back inside and began firing again, first at the victims and then indiscriminately into the dance floor.[10] Marcelle Ford died on the way to the hospital. Belachheb later called police and admitted to the shooting and was arrested.

RUN/HIDE/Fight

Witness Terry Rippa said he was just reaching for money to pay his bar bill when he heard the gunshots. "We went under the table, and the guy went one, two, three, four, five down the row," Rippa said.[11]

Some 20 people fled the restaurant through the back door and hid behind wide pillars holding up the breezeway.[12]

Run/Hide/Fight/OTHER
Ran toward shooter trying to stop him

Patron Frank Parker was in the kitchen when the shooting started. Unarmed, Parker ran out the back kitchen door toward Belachheb. A witness stated, "Parker was coming from the back of the restaurant to the front... [he] got hit and it kind of stood him up, and then he got [shot] twice more and it dropped him..." Parker died almost immediately.[13]

Case #4 – McDonald's Restaurant

Synopsis	James Oliver Huberty, 41, opened fire in a McDonald's restaurant before he was shot dead by a police sniper.
Type of Establishment	Restaurant
Environment	Indoors and outdoors
Motive	Revenge
Number killed	21
Number killed and injured	40
Date of murders	July 18, 1984
Weapons	9mm Uzi semi-automatic; Winchester pump-action 12-gauge shotgun; 9mm Browning HP semi-automatic handgun
Location	San Ysidro, California
Shooter status	Fatally shot by SWAT team sniper the same day

Overview

James Oliver Huberty, age 41, had a history of violent behavior and domestic violence. In early 1984 the Huberty family moved from Ohio to California, where James found a job as a security guard in San Ysidro. He was dismissed from the position in early July. On July 18, Huberty called a mental health center for an appointment to try to deal with his anger, but did not receive a return call.[14]

The next day he told his wife he was going to "hunt humans." Carrying an Uzi semi-automatic rifle, a shotgun, a pistol, and a bag of ammunition, he walked from his house to a busy McDonald's restaurant. A witness spotted Huberty carrying the firearms and called police, but the dispatcher gave officers the wrong address.[15]

Entering the restaurant, Huberty ordered those inside to lie prone and began shooting, and continued shooting for more than an hour. He fired at adults and children outside the restaurant as well. A police officer said that the gunman had "a couple of rifles and immediately started shooting everything he could shoot...when we arrived here...the first police vehicle and fire vehicle were both fired upon."[16] When an employee picked up a telephone to call the police, the gunman began firing at those on the floor.

Police initially responded to a McDonald's near the U.S. border with Tijuana, and 15 minutes later learned the correct location of the shooting about two miles away. After expending more than 250 rounds of ammunition, Huberty was fatally shot by a police sniper positioned on a rooftop across the street.

By the time the shooting ended, there were 21 dead and 19 wounded. Huberty's victims ranged in age from 6 months to 74 years of age.[17]

Run/HIDE/Fight

When the shooting started, college student employee Ken Dickey and a co-worker fled to a basement utility room, where they were joined by three female co-workers, a woman with a baby, and a man who was bleeding. They huddled in the hot basement with gunfire sounding overhead. Finally, police knocked at the door, and though they were fearful, they opened it.[18]

RUN/HIDE/Fight

Huberty jumped over the counter to check the kitchen and found Guillermo Flores on the floor talking to police. Also present were grill workers Alex Vasquez and Albert Leos, and three female counter workers. "Oh," Huberty observed calmly, "there's more." He cried, "You're trying to hide from me, you bastards!" and raised the Uzi. One of the women screamed in Spanish: "Don't kill me! Don't kill me!", but Huberty opened fire. The three men jumped up to flee; Flores and Vasquez were able to escape. Albert Leos tried to run, but one of the women grabbed him and pulled him down and he was caught in the line of fire. Wounded but still alive, he crawled to the shelter of a table, but the three female employees were dead.[19]

Run/Hide/Fight/OTHER
Drew gunman's attention

An 11-year-old girl lay on the restaurant floor with her eyes closed tight in fear. "I thought I heard him far away, so I opened my eyes and he saw me. He walked to the trash can and he had some [guns] in there. He got his shotgun. That's when he shot me."[20]

Run/Hide/Fight/OTHER
Played dead

11-year-old Joshua Coleman had ridden his bicycle to McDonald's to get a soft drink. He was on the sidewalk when Joshua heard the man yell. He turned and was hit. Lying on the pavement, his right side riddled with shotgun pellets, and the gunman still shooting, Joshua played dead. How did he know to do so? "I don't know," he says. "I got lucky...You hear about an accident and sometimes you think, 'What would you do if you were there?' and I always thought I would play dead.[21]

Run/Hide/Fight/OTHER
Confronted gunman

Huberty discharged a round into the ceiling when he entered the restaurant. Restaurant manager Neva Caine got out of her booth and went to confront the man. Huberty shot once at point-blank range and Caine died within minutes.[22]

Mass Shootings

Mass Shootings

Case #5 – U.S. Postal Service

Synopsis	Postal worker Patrick Sherrill, 44, opened fire at a post office before committing suicide.
Type of Establishment	Workplace
Environment	Indoors
Motive	Revenge
Number killed	14
Number killed and injured	20
Date of murders	August 20, 1986
Weapons	Two .45 caliber semi-automatic pistols; .22 caliber handgun
Location	Edmond, Oklahoma
Shooter status	Committed suicide by shooting himself the same day

Overview

Patrick Henry Sherrill was a loner whose neighbors called him "Crazy Pat" due to a long history of bizarre behavior.[23] After 16 months on the job as a permanent part-time letter carrier, he had been reprimanded by two supervisors about misdirected mail and tardy performance. Sherill reported to a postal union steward that he was being mistreated. "I gotta get out of here," he said.[24]

At about 7:00 a.m. on August 20, Sherrill entered the post office from the employee parking lot, carrying three pistols and ammunition in a mailbag on his shoulder. Without saying a word, he gunned down one of the supervisors who had criticized him, as well as a fellow postman. He fired at fleeing employees and at workers hiding under tables and in cubicles. Within minutes, 12 more were dead and six wounded.[25]

Police arrived on scene just minutes after the shooting began. They attempted for 45 minutes to communicate with Sherrill by telephone and bullhorn, without response. When a SWAT team stormed the building at 8:30 a.m., they found the gunman's body, dead of a bullet to the head.[26] Sherill's rampage had lasted between 15 and 20 minutes.[27]

RUN/Hide/Fight

Sherrill chased some fleeing employees out a side exit, shooting one man, who later died in the parking lot.[28]

Employee Debbie Smith was sorting letters when the shooting began. "I froze. I couldn't run." As she hid, Sherrill passed her and opened fire on the next section. Smith ran for the front door and escaped.[29]

RUN/HIDE/Fight

Richard Tompkins said, "I ran around behind some rural carrier cases trying to hide. When it got quiet I headed for the back door...the shooting started again toward the front of the post office, so I went to the back and got a door open."[30]

Peggy Gibson was nearly killed. "I hid under my case and behind the parcel tub. I ran to the back doors [found locked] ... then ran to the side door and outside."[31]

Darrell Fesler saw what was happening. "I heard a gunshot, and hid behind some big boxes. I looked up and saw a man shooting a gun. He shot Mike Bigler and then just turned in a circle shooting at random. He went towards the front lobby shooting and we ran out the back. He followed, still firing, and then returned inside."[32]

Run/HIDE/Fight
Hid in vault

Another employee escaped by locking herself in a vault where stamps are kept.[33]

Run/HIDE/Fight
Hid in closet

Tracy Sanchez "ran to the back door, but it was locked. Another man tried to get out with me. We ran back and there was a storage closet nearby. We hid in there, but we couldn't lock it so we turned the lights off and stayed quiet. Sherrill stood by our door and kept emptying his shells and reloading his gun...Then, finally, it got quiet. But we stayed hidden until we heard the police."[34]

Run/HIDE/Fight
Hid in open area

Sherrill bolted several doors and then systematically searched the workroom floor for workers who were cowering under tables and in cubicles. He killed three people in one work station and five in another.[35]

Run/Hide/FIGHT

Employee Larry Wilson tried to stop the slaughter. He said, "I kicked the gun out of Pat's hand but he recovered it and started shooting again."[36]

Run/Hide/Fight/OTHER
Played dead

Mike Bigler survived by playing dead. He was heading toward an exit and was shot in the back... "I just played dead. Sherrill kept walking around several times...just went around shooting methodically, saying nothing."[37]

Mass Shootings

Case #6 – Shopping Centers

Synopsis	William Cruse, 58, killed six strangers at two shopping centers.
Type of Establishment	Shopping centers
Environment	Outdoors/indoors
Motive	Revenge/rampage
Number killed	6
Number killed and injured	20
Date of murders	April 23, 1987
Weapons	Assault rifle; shotgun; pistol
Location	Palm Bay, Florida
Shooter status	Sentenced to death on July 28, 1989; died on death row in 2009

Overview

On the afternoon of April 23, 1987, carrying a shotgun, retired librarian William Cruse charged out of his house to confront some teens who were bouncing a basketball in a neighbor's driveway. He fired at and wounded a 14-year-old. Then he drove away, firing at neighbors' homes as he drove. He fired at two Florida Tech students and killed them; then he shot and injured two other men. Arriving at a Publix supermarket, Cruse shot and killed a woman leaving the store.[38]

Cruse then drove to a Winn Dixie supermarket. As he was firing at the store, police officer Ronald Grogan approached in his car; Cruse fired numerous shots into the car, killing the officer.[39] Officer Gerald Johnson arrived on scene next. Cruse shot the officer in the leg. Johnson emptied his gun at Cruse but missed. As he tried to reload, Cruse shot him and killed him.[40]

Cruse continued shooting at anyone he saw. As police surrounded the store, he found two women hiding in the restroom and took one of them hostage. After several hours, he let her go, at which time police fired tear gas and stun grenades into the store.[41] Cruse was arrested shortly afterward.

Run/HIDE/Fight

Police found three people huddled unhurt in a refrigerated storeroom.[42]

Run/Hide/FIGHT

Just before he killed the officer, Cruse took aim at customer Ruben Torres. "I looked toward the glass doors, and I guess William Cruse saw me because he shot at me right through the doors and everything I had in my hand went flying," Torres recalled. "After that I crawled up to the window and saw him walking across the parking lot. I don't know where I got the strength from, but I took the doors off the track and got out of the store." [43]

As Cruse killed Officer Johnson, Torres ran to his car and "I got my gun out of my glove compartment and we started a little shootout," he said. "I was shooting at him and he was shooting at me." When Torres went back to his car for more ammunition, a police officer stopped him, thinking he was a second gunman. Torres was later credited with distracting Cruse, allowing people to escape from the grocery store. [44]

Run/Hide/Fight/OTHER
Hostage response

Robin Brown, 21, held hostage for six hours, communicated with the shooter. She says she wiped blood from the gunman's hands, helped him smash store lights, and fed him potato chips. "I tried to get him to surrender. I stopped him from killing himself and from killing me."[45]

Case #7 – ELECTROMAGNETIC SYSTEMS LAB

Synopsis	Silicon Valley defense plant employee Richard Wade Farley, 39, shot and killed seven and wounded four more at his company's office.
Type of Establishment	Workplace
Environment	Indoors and outdoors
Motive	Revenge after being spurned
Number killed	7
Number killed and injured	11
Date of murders	February 16, 1988
Weapons	Benelli semi-automatic shotgun; pump-action shotgun; rifle; four handguns
Location	Sunnyvale, California
Shooter status	In December 1991, sentenced to death in gas chamber; ruling upheld in July 2009.[46]

Overview

At Electromagnetic Systems Lab (ESL), Richard Wade Farley was obsessed with co-worker Laura Black and had stalked her for several years. In the autumn of 1985 the Human Resources department of the company ordered Farley to attended counseling sessions; he did so, but continued the harassment of Black. By the following spring Farley was threatening fellow employees. That along with his poor work performance resulted in his termination in May of 1986. Even after his employment at another company, he continued his stalking. Black was granted a temporary restraining order against Farley, and he was ordered to leave her alone pending a full hearing on February 17, 1988.[47]

On February 16, Farley drove to the ESL parking lot with a "Benelli semi-automatic shotgun, a rifle with a scope, a pump-action shotgun, a Sentinal revolver, a Smith & Wesson .357 Magnum revolver, a Browning semi-automatic pistol, a Smith & Wesson pistol, a smoke bomb, a belt with pouches filled with ammunition, other bags containing more than 200 rounds of ammunition, and a vest containing more than 800 rounds of ammunition...a foot-long buck knife and sheath, and ear protectors."[48] He walked into a side door by shooting the glass, and continued shooting as he headed to Black's second-floor office. When he reached the office she slammed the door, but he fired through the door. The first shot missed but the second hit her in the shoulder and she fell to the floor unconscious.

Farley held a police SWAT team at bay for five hours, speaking on the telephone numerous times with the hostage negotiator. He eventually surrendered to police. He had expended 98 rounds of ammunition.[49] Seven people lay dead, and four more were wounded.

In October of 1991 Farley was convicted of seven counts of first-degree murder, and later sentenced to death.

Run/HIDE/Fight

Lisa Black awakened after being shot, and she and other survivors hid from Farley while he was holding the SWAT team at bay. They later escaped.[50]

Run/HIDE/Fight/OTHER
Released by gunman

Linda Walden, the shooter's friend and former landlady, was hiding under the desk at which Farley was standing while he was on the telephone with police. He pulled out the desk chair and saw her and said, "Oh, there's someone here. You can come out now. Oh, it's Linda." When she emerged Farley told her she could leave. Employee Christine Hansen, hiding nearby, thought the police were evacuating the building and she came out of hiding. When she saw Farley she asked if she could leave, too, and he told her, "Yes, you can go."[51]

Case #8 – CLEVELAND ELEMENTARY SCHOOL

Synopsis	Patrick Purdy, 26, launched an assault at Cleveland Elementary School, where many young Southeast Asian immigrants were enrolled. Purdy then committed suicide.
Type of Establishment	School
Environment	Outdoors
Motive	Racial
Number killed	5
Number killed and injured	35
Date of murders	January 17, 1989
Weapons	AK-47-type semi-automatic assault rifle; two handguns
Location	Stockton, California
Shooter status	Committed suicide by shooting himself in the head the same day

Overview

On January 17, 1989, at 11.40 a.m., former Stockton resident Patrick Purdy, a disturbed loner with guerrilla-warfare fantasies[52], parked his car outside the Cleveland Elementary School, got out, set it alight by means of a gasoline-filled beer bottle, and walked toward the school. Some 300 pupils were outside at recess.

Purdy was dressed in battle gear and wearing a flak jacket. He entered the school grounds through a gap in the fence carrying two handguns and an AK-47. He opened fire at a group of portable classrooms, and moved away and fired across the blacktop where children were playing, toward the main building about 250 yards away. A number of rounds went completely through the main school building and came out the other side.[53]

When the four-minute assault ended, five young children were dead; one teacher and 29 pupils were wounded.[54]

The dead were all Southeast Asians from war-refugee groups which comprised more than 70% of the school's enrollment. A report to the California Attorney General indicated that Purdy blamed all minorities for his failings, and "selected Southeast Asians because they were the minority with whom he was most in contact."[55]

Run/HIDE/Fight

Teacher Lori Mackey said she ran to her classroom window when she heard what she thought were firecrackers, and when she realized what was happening, she took her 10 pupils into a rear room where they could not be seen.[56]

Case #9 – STANDARD GRAVURE PRINTING CO.

Synopsis	Joseph T. Wesbecker, 47, gunned down eight people at his former workplace before committing suicide.
Type of Establishment	Workplace
Environment	Indoors
Motive	Revenge
Number killed	8
Number killed and injured	20
Date of murders	September 14, 1989
Weapons	AK-47 semi-automatic rifle; two MAC-11 semi-automatic pistols; .38 caliber revolver; 9mm automatic pistol; bayonet
Location	Louisville, Kentucky
Shooter status	Committed suicide by shooting himself the same day

Overview

Joseph Wesbecker had worked for printing company Standard Gravure for 17 years, but went on disability leave in the spring of 1989 as a result of mental illness. He had a history of suicide attempts.

On September 14, 1989 at about 8:30 a.m., Wesbecker entered the Standard Gravure plant carrying a duffel bag containing an AK-47 semi-automatic rifle, two MAC-11 semi-automatic pistols, a .38-caliber revolver, a 9mm automatic pistol, and a bayonet, along with thousands of rounds of ammunition.[57] He took the elevator to the executive reception area and, as soon as the doors opened, fired at receptionists Sharon Needy, killing her, and Angela Bowman, leaving her paralyzed by a shot in the back. Searching for Michael Shea, president of Standard Gravure, and other supervisors and bosses of the plant, Wesbecker calmly walked through the hallways, deliberately shooting at people.[58]

Wesbacker eventually went to the pressroom, put a gun under his chin, and killed himself. He had killed seven people and wounded 13.

Run/HIDE/Fight

Employee John Tingle encountered Wesbecker at the beginning of the rampage. Wesbecker said to him, "I told them I'd be back. Get out of my way, John." "{Tingle} said, 'How are you, Rock?'" He said, "Fine, John. Back off and get out of my way." Tingle and other nearby employees fled to a restroom and locked the door.[59]

Mass Shootings

Case Studies - 1990s

Case #10 – GENERAL MOTORS ACCEPTANCE CORP.

Synopsis	James Edward Pough, 42, opened fire at an auto loan company office before committing suicide.
Type of Establishment	Business
Environment	Indoors
Motive	Revenge
Number killed	9
Number killed and injured	13
Date of murders	June 18, 1990
Weapons	.30 caliber M1 assault rifle; .38 revolver (9mm semi-automatic left in car)
Location	Jacksonville, Florida
Shooter status	Committed suicide by shooting himself the same day

Overview

James Edward Pough's car had been repossessed by General Motors Acceptance Corporation in January of 1990, and he later received a bill for more than $6,000 in outstanding charges.[60] Besides his financial problems, his marriage had apparently broken up that month, and his wife had obtained a protective order to keep him away from her for a year.[61]

On June 17 of that year, Pough killed a pimp and a prostitute who were standing on a corner not far from his home in Jacksonville. About ten minutes after those murders Pough shot and wounded two youths, 17 and 18 years of age, after asking them for directions.[62]

The next morning, Pough drove to the GMAC office. Leaving a 9mm semi-automatic pistol in the trunk of his Buick, he entered the building through the front door, and without saying a word, immediately began shooting with an M1 carbine, killing customer Julia Burgess at the front counter.[63]

David Hendricks, 26, was standing at the counter making a payment when he heard a worker scream. At that instant, he was shot in the back. As he turned, Pough fired three more shots into him.[64]

As Pough walked through the office, he moved from desk to desk, shooting at employees hiding underneath.[65] Pough had killed nine and wounded four more. He then shot and killed himself.

RUN/Hide/Fight

When the GMAC employees realized what was happening, many of them were able to escape through a back door of the building.[66]

Run/HIDE/Fight

When someone hollered "Get down!" some in the office realized what was happening and dived under desks, and were trapped there. Pough began picking off persons who were ducking for cover, and shot at least eight people one by one. All those killed were shot two to four times, mostly as they crouched under their desks in an attempt to hide.[67]

Case #11 - Luby's Cafeteria

Synopsis	George Hennard, 35, drove his pickup into a cafeteria and opened fire on those inside before committing suicide.
Type of Establishment	Business
Environment	Indoors
Motive	Revenge
Number killed	23
Number killed and injured	50
Date of murders	October 16, 1991
Weapons	Glock 17 pistol; Ruger P89 pistol
Location	Killeen, Texas
Shooter status	Committed suicide by shooting himself in the head after being cornered and wounded by police the same day

Overview

On October 16, 1991, George Hennard drove his pickup truck through the front window of the Luby's Cafeteria and, armed with two semi-automatic pistols, began firing at those inside. Most of his victims were women. Hennard shouted, "All women of Killeen and Belton are vipers! See what you've done to me and my family!" As he continued shooting, often at point-blank range into the victim's head, he yelled, "Is it worth it? Tell me, is it worth it?"[68]

By the time police arrived, Hennard had killed 22 (one died later) and wounded 27. He exchanged gunfire with officers for a few minutes, then ran toward the restrooms and shot himself in the head. The entire incident had lasted only about 10 minutes.[69]

RUN/Hide/Fight

Seventy-one-year-old Hazel Holley broke her arm as she escaped through a broken window.[70] The gunman faced down another patron, Sam Wink, but when a woman nearby tried to run away he was distracted and fired at her, which allowed Wink to flee.[71]

Run/HIDE/Fight

The attack was so sudden and terrifying that patrons and restaurant workers could only duck under tables, chairs and benches, clasping hands and praying.[72] One woman survived by hiding in a freezer; she was later treated for hypothermia.[73]

Food preparer Mark Matthews, age 19, escaped by hiding inside an industrial dishwasher. He was so frightened that he did not come out until the following day.[74]

RUN/Hide/Fight/OTHER
Helped others

Customer Tommy Vaughn, 6'6" and 300 lbs. in weight, threw himself through the front window and broke it, allowing others to escape. Within moments, dozens of people were pushing, shoving and knocking each other down as they made their escape.[75]

Run/Hide/Fight/OTHER
Gunman allowed two to leave

The gunman allowed a mother and her four-year-old child to leave. In his only show of mercy, he pointed a pistol at a blood-splattered Anica McNeil, who'd just seen her mother shot dead and said, "You with the baby, get out."[76]

Case #12 – UNIVERSITY OF IOWA

Synopsis	Former graduate student Gang Lu, 28, went on a rampage on campus and then committed suicide.
Type of Establishment	School/university
Environment	Indoors
Motive	Revenge
Number killed	5
Number killed and injured	6
Date of murders	November 1, 1991
Weapons	.38 caliber revolver; .22 caliber handgun
Location	Iowa City, Iowa
Shooter status	Committed suicide by shooting himself the same day

Overview

Gang Lu, born in Beijing, China, was a graduate student in physics at the University of Iowa who had received his doctoral degree from that university the previous May. Gang was upset that his dissertation was not awarded a prestigious dissertation prize which incuded a monetary award, which prize was instead awarded to student Linhua Chan.[77]

On November 1, 1991, at about 3:40 in the afternoon, Gang attended a physics and astronomy department meeting. Shortly after the meeting began, he pulled a revolver from his jacket and began shooting. He killed the department chair and two professors (all of whom had been involved in Gang's doctoral work), and then shot and killed rival Linhua Shan.[78]

Gang left the building, crossed two streets, entered another building and went to the second floor. He shot and killed the associate vice president for academic affairs (whose office had denied the

Mass Shootings

dissertation prize), and shot and wounded a student working in the office.[79]

Entering an empty conference room, Gang took off his jacket, folded it, and then killed himself, 12 minutes after he had fired the first shot.[80]

Run/HIDE/Fight

As students scrambled to find cover, one crawled under a table but was shot in the hand and chest.[81]

Case #13 – Lindhurst High School

Synopsis	Former student Eric Houston, 20, killed three students and a teacher and wounded 10 others at Lindhurst High School before surrendering to police after an eight-hour standoff.
Type of Establishment	School
Environment	Indoors
Motive	Revenge
Number killed	4
Number killed and injured	13
Date of murders	May 1, 1992
Weapons	12-gauge pump-action shotgun; sawed-off .22 caliber rifle
Location	Olivehurst, California
Shooter status	Sentenced to death in September 1993; sentence upheld by California Supreme Court in 2012.[82]

Overview

20-year-old Eric Houston was a former student at Lindhurst High School. He had not graduated from the school due to a failing grade from his Civics teacher.[83]

On May 1, 1992, at just before 3:00 p.m., Houston came to the school campus armed with a a 12-gauge pump-action shotgun and a sawed off .22 caliber rifle, wearing military camouflage with bandoliers across his chest.[84] As he entered the school, he fatally shot teacher Robert Brens, who had been Houston's Civics teacher his senior year. He then shot and killed Judy Davis, a student who was inside Brens' classroom.[85]

Houston then walked through the hallway outside the classroom and fatally shot student Jason Edward White in the chest. Houston pointed his shotgun at a female student, but before he could fire his weapon another student, Beamon A. Hill, pushed her aside and took the shotgun blast to the side of his head.[86]

Houston then entered a classroom with about 25 to 30 students inside. He sent a student to retrieve more hostages, and eventually held more than 80 students hostage. After negotiations with police, he released some of the hostages. He surrendered to police after an eight-hour standoff.[87]

Run/HIDE/Fight

Johnny Mills recalled that "our teacher...poked his head out the door to see what the ruckus was and immediately slammed the door shut and yelled, 'Get down! Get down!' Now we all looked at him In shock and he said, 'They are shooting! Get down!' I dove to the ground and crawled to the back of the right stage and huddled in the corner.[88]

Sophomore Jennifer Thompson said she heard shots in bursts. "Bang, bang, bang. Silence, then again," she said, adding that her teacher first thought it was firecrackers. Then students slid under their desks as they had been trained to do.[89]

Case #14 – Law Firm Office Building

Synopsis	Businessman Gian Luigi Ferri, 55, opened fire throughout an office building before committing suicide inside as police pursued him.
Type of Establishment	Business
Environment	Indoors
Motive	Uncertain; suspected revenge
Number killed	8
Number killed and injured	14
Date of murders	July 1, 1993
Weapons	Two TEC-9 semi-automatic handguns; .45 semi-automatic pistol
Location	San Francisco, California
Shooter status	Committed suicide by shooting himself the same day

Overview

Gian Luigi Ferri was apparently dissatisfied with the legal services he had received from the law firm of Pettit & Martin. At just before 3:00 p.m. on July 1, 1993, he entered the firm's office building and made his way to the 34th floor where the firm was officed. Exiting the elevator, Ferri opened fire with a pair of TEC-9 handguns and a .45 pistol. After roaming the floor he took the stairs down one flight and continued shooting. Eight people were killed in the attack and six others were injured.[90]

RUN/HIDE/Fight

The gunman fired through the conference room's glass window, killing two people on the spot. One woman hid under a table, and another ran for her life, while being shot five times.[91]

Down the hall, John Scully heard the shooting and ran down a staircase to an empty office on the 33rd floor where his wife was. They ran toward the elevator to escape but were confronted by the gunman. As Ferri aimed, Scully put himself in front of his wife and was fatally wounded.[92]

Run/HIDE/OTHER
Verbally engaged with gunman

Survivor Charles Ross said that "The gunman was cold, detached, impassive as if I could be anybody. It made me realize that I had to be as cold-blooded to him as he was to me." Ross slammed his door shut, but Ferri opened it. Ross yelled "Who the hell are you?" and pushed past the gunman and ran down two corridors, then ducked into a room to hide.[93]

Case #15 – LUIGI'S RESTAURANT

Synopsis	Army Sgt. Kenneth Junior French, 22, opened fire inside an Italian restaurant while ranting about gays in the military, before he was shot and arrested by police.
Type of Establishment	Restaurant
Environment	Indoors
Motive	Unknown
Number killed	4
Number killed and injured	12
Date of murders	August 6, 1993
Weapons	Pump shotgun
Location	Fayetteville, North Carolina
Shooter status	Sentenced to four consecutive life terms plus 35 years in 1994.

Overview

On the night of August 6, 1993, Kenneth Junior French got out of a truck near Luigi's Restaurant and a Kroger supermarket in Fayetteville, North Carolina. Wearing a hunting vest and carrying a pump shotgun, he began firing toward the Kroger store. He then walked to the back of the restaurant and entered through the kitchen area. Hollering "freeze," French walked through the restaurant and killed four people and wounded others, often firing right in people's faces after they asked for mercy.[94]

Witnesses reported that during the shootings, French shouted, "I'll show you, Clinton, about letting gays into the army."[95] French claimed that before the rampage, he had consumed about a fifth of whiskey while watching the movie "The Unforgiven," which includes a scene of a violent massacre at a saloon.[96]

Mass Shootings

A Fayetteville police officer was working off-duty at Kroger and heard the shots. He called for backup, entered Luigi's, and shot French. Another officer approached and French raised his gun; the second officer fired twice. The shotgun was taken from French and he was arrested and taken to a hospital for surgery. Four people were dead and eight more were wounded.

RUN/HIDE/Fight

As the shooting began, restaurant patrons began running out the door and hiding under tables.[97]

Run/Hide/Fight/OTHER
Protected loved ones

Restaurant patron James Kidd hid in a booth and covered his son. The gunman shot Kidd, who died almost immediately. The son was not physically harmed.[98]

Run/Hide/Fight/OTHER
Drew attention of the shooter

Restaurant cook Willie McCormick was the first person shot when he tried to walk away from the gunman, but he survived.

Restaurant proprietor Pete Parrous approached French and asked him not to hurt anyone. Parrous was shot in the face and died instantly. As he fell, his wife stood up screaming and French shot her. Mrs. Parrous fell beside her daughter, who began screaming and who was shot in the thigh.

Wesley Cover had been tending to a patron who had been hit by a pellet from the shooting. He asked the gunman not to hurt the woman he was helping because she was pregnant. Mr. Cover was then shot in the head and died. The woman was also shot, but not fatally.[99]

Mass Shootings

Case #16 – LONG ISLAND RAILROAD

Synopsis	Colin Ferguson, 35, opened fire on a commuter train from New York City's Pennsylvania Station. He was tackled by three passengers when he stopped to reload.
Type of Establishment	Commuter train
Environment	Indoors
Motive	Racial
Number killed	6
Number killed and injured	25
Date of murders	December 7, 1993
Weapons	Ruger P89 9mm semi-automatic pistol
Location	Long Island, New York
Shooter status	Sentenced to six consecutive 25-years-to-life terms on February 17, 1995

Overview

On December 7, 1993, Colin Ferguson purchased a ticket at Pennsylvania Station in New York City and boarded the third car of the eastbound Long Island Railroad 5:33 evening commuter train to Hicksville, along with 80 other passengers. Ferguson sat at the western end of the car, carrying a handgun and a canvas bag filled with 160 rounds of ammunition.[100]

As the train approached the Merillon Avenue Station, Ferguson drew the gun, dropped several cartridges on the ground, stood up and started opening fire on the passengers at random, but apparently targeting white people.[101] He was finally tackled and held by passengers until he could be arrested.

Colin defended himself at his trial claiming that he was the victim of a racist conspiracy.[102] In February 1995 he was convicted and sentenced to six consecutive 25-years-to-life sentences.

RUN/Hide/Fight

The train's engineer learned of the shooting but he decided against opening the train doors because two of the cars were not yet at the platform. Although an announcement was made ordering conductors not to open the doors, one conductor climbed out of a train window and opened a door of the third car from the outside so that passengers could escape.[103]

RUN/HIDE/Fight

Ferguson walked east on the train, pulling the trigger steadily about every half second. Some passengers tried to hide underneath the seats; others ran to the eastern end of the train and tried to go into the next car.[104]

Run/HIDE/Fight

At the front of the car, William Warshowsky was waiting by the door as the train approached the station when he heard the pop of the 9-millimeter gunfire and mistook it for something harmless, caps or fireworks. "A woman yelled, 'He's got a gun! He's shooting people!' " the passenger recalled. He jumped down into a seat to hide as the bullets sprayed about the car.[105]

Run/Hide/FIGHT

Ferguson emptied two 15-round magazines during the shooting. As he was reloading a third magazine, passengers Michael O'Connor, Kevin Blum and Mark McEntee tackled the gunman and pinned him to one of the train's seats. Other passengers ran to grab his arms and legs and help hold him down. Andrew Roderick, an off-duty Long Island Rail Road policeman, boarded the train car and handcuffed Ferguson.[106]

Run/Hide/Fight/OTHER
Played dead

The first gunshot victim, Mary Anne Phillips, testified that she had played dead after being wounded. She said she kept her eyes closed so that Ferguson would not come back and shoot her again."[107]

Mass Shootings

Case #17 – Chuck E. Cheese Restaurant

Synopsis	Nathan Dunlap, 33, went on a rampage through his former workplace and was arrested the following day.
Type of Establishment	Restaurant
Environment	Indoors
Motive	Revenge/robbery
Number killed	4
Number killed and injured	5
Date of murders	December 14, 1993
Weapons	Small caliber semi-automatic handgun
Location	Aurora, Colorado
Shooter status	Sentenced to death on May 17, 1996. At publication time, he is on death row awaiting execution. In February 2013 the U.S. Supreme Court delined to hear his appeal.[108]

Overview

On the night of December 14, 1993, Nathan Dunlap entered the Chuck E Cheese restaurant from which he had recently been dismissed as a kitchen worker. He ordered a sandwich, played a video game, and then hid in the restroom until closing. When employees were cleaning up, he confronted and shot two workers, shot a third one in a hallway, shot and wounded another in the kitchen, before robbing and killing the manager in her office.[109] Then he grabbed her bag, filled it with game tokens, key chains, cards, $1,591 and change, and shot her again.

Employee Sylvia Crowell was cleaning the salad bar when Dunlap came up behind her. He raised his pistol to her left ear and pulled the trigger. Employee Ben Grant, a high school junior, was vacuuming. Dunlap shot him in the face and killed him.[110]

Mass Shootings

The shooting spree lasted only about five minutes. Dunlap was arrested about 12 hours after the murders.[111]

RUN/Hide/Fight

After being shot, Bobby Stevens fled the restaurant and ran to nearby apartments to call the police.[112]

Run/Hide/Fight/OTHER
Pled for life

Colleen O'Connor saw Dunlap coming and knelt in front of him to beg for her life. As she raised her arms, he held a gun just 18 inches from her head. "Don't shoot," she cried. "I won't tell." "I have to," the shooter said as he pulled the trigger.[113]

Case #18 – FAIRCHILD AIR FORCE BASE

Synopsis	Former airman Dean Allen Mellberg, 20, opened fire inside a hospital at the Fairchild Air Force Base before he was shot dead by a military police officer.
Type of Establishment	Air Force Base hospital
Environment	Indoors
Motive	Revenge
Number killed	4
Number killed and injured	26
Date of murders	June 20, 1994
Weapons	Chinese-made MAK-90 assault rifle
Location	Spokane County, Washington
Shooter status	Shot and killed by military police officer

Overview

Dean A. Mellberg had been discharged from the U.S. Air Force for chronic problems. Major Thomas E. Brigham, psychiatrist, and Captain Alan W. London, psychologist, had both recommended his discharge. On June 21, 1994, Mellberg entered the Fairchild Air Force Base hospital annex carrying a duffel bag containing a Chinese-made MAK-90 assault rifle. He went to a restroom inside the hospital's annex, where he removed the rifle from the duffel bag. He the went to the office shared by Maj. Brigham and Capt. London, and killed them both with two bursts of gunfire.[114]

Mellberg then proceeded down the corridors of the annex and sprayed them with round after round as panic-stricken patients and medical personnel ran for their lives. He then entered the adjoining main hospital building and began shooting in the cafeteria.[115]

Mass Shootings

After several minutes inside the annex and the main building, Mr. Mellberg left and went to the parking lot, where he killed Anita Linder, the 62-year-old wife of a retired serviceman.

Senior Airman Andrew Brown with the security police was patrolling on a bicycle when he received an emergency call on his radio. He rode a quarter-mile to the scene, and spotted Mellberg shooting in the parking lot. Brown ordered the gunman to drop his weapon; Mellberg turned and shot at the officer. Brown returned fire, killing the gunman with two shots to the head.[116]

Run/Hide/Fight/OTHER
Gunman's choice

As Mellberg burst through the door of the office shared by Maj. Brigham and Capt. London, Tiffany Williams was just finishing her therapy session with Capt. London. Mellberg shot London in the chest. He aimed the rifle at Williams, they locked eyes, then Mellberg turned and left. Williams immediately called 911 and reported the shooting.[117]

Case #19 – WALTER ROSSLER CO.

Synopsis	Former metallurgist James Daniel Simpson, 28, opened fire throughout the company where he had worked, killing five before committing suicide.
Type of Establishment	Business
Environment	Indoors
Motive	Unknown (mental illness)
Number killed	5
Number killed and injured	5
Date of murders	April 3, 1995
Weapons	Ruger 9mm pistol; .32 revolver
Location	Corpus Christi, Texas
Shooter status	Committed suicide by shooting himself the same day

Overview

28-year-old James Simpson had worked for a year as a metallurgist at the Walter Rossler Co., a refinery inspection company in Corpus Christi, Texas, before quitting in September 1994.

On April 3, 1995, he walked into the company through the front door; carrying a 9mm semi-automatic pistol and a .32 caliber revolver. He walked up to employee Wendy Gilmore, said, "This is for you, bitch," and shot her. He then shot owner Walter Rossler and Rossler's wife Joan, and two other employees. The gunman then walked out the back door and shot himself behind the building as police closed in.[118]

According to police, the motive for the shooting was Simpson's apparent depression.[119]

RUN/Hide/Fight

As Simpson shot Wendy Gilmore, Joan Rossler and the other secretary ran. Rossler was shot and killed.[120]

Run/**HIDE**/Fight

Lisa Rossler-Duff, daughter of the company's owners, grabbed her 8-month-old-son and crawled under a desk, then ran to another office and called 911.[121]

Mass Shootings

Case #20 - FREDDIE'S FASHION MART

Synopsis	Roland J. Smith, 51, opened fire inside a Harlem clothing store, also setting it on fire, then committed suicide.
Type of Establishment	Business
Environment	Indoors
Motive	Racial
Number killed	7
Number killed and injured	11
Date of murders	December 8, 1995
Weapons	Gun (and fire causing death by smoke inhalation)
Location	Harlem, New York City, New York
Shooter status	Committed suicide by shooting himself the same day

Overview

Freddie's Fashion Mart, a Jewish-owned business located across the street from the famous Apollo Theater, had been picketed for weeks in a dispute over the rent raise to a subtenant, the black-owned Record Shack. The picketers claimed that Freddie's did not employ blacks and was behind the threatened eviction of the Record Shack.[122]

On December 8, at 10:12 a.m., Roland James Smith, Jr., a Harlem resident with a criminal record going back 30 years who had been among the picketers, walked into Freddie's, pulled out a gun, shouted for people to get out, kicked over a table, spilled paint thinner on several bins of clothing and set them on fire, and began shooting.[123]

After exchanging gunfire with police, Smith set several fires in the store. The intensity of the fire prevented police and firefighters from gaining access inside the store for more than two hours. They found three bodies huddled together in a back room on the first floor and four more in the basement. Seven of the victims apparently died of smoke inhalation.[124]

Smith was found dead inside with a gun in his hand.

RUN/Hide/Fight

Four wounded people managed to stumble out of the store before the fire enveloped it.[125]

Case #21 – MUNICIPAL OFFICE

Synopsis	Fired city park employee Clifton McCree, 41, opened fire on former coworkers inside their municipal trailer, then committed suicide.
Type of Establishment	Government office
Environment	Indoors
Motive	Revenge/racial
Number killed	5
Number killed and injured	6
Date of murders	February 9, 1996
Weapon	Glock 9mm semi-automatic pistol
Location	Fort Lauderdale, Florida
Shooter status	Committed suicide by shooting himself the same day

Overview

Clifton McCree had worked for the city of Fort Lauderdale park department for 18 years. He was fired for rudeness to the public, threatening co-workers, and failing a drug test. He threatened to return to his workplace and "do things."[126]

Fourteen months later, at 5:00 a.m. on February 9, 1996, McCree went to a temporary trailer office a block from the beach and systematically began firing on the beach cleaning crew he once worked with as they sat around a table preparing for work. Armed with a .9mm semi-automatic handgun, he burst through the door and said "Everyone's going to die," then pulled out a 9mm semi-automatic pistol and began shooting, killing five co-workers and critically wounding another. He then turned the gun on himself and committed suicide. A suicide note he left behind stated that the shootings were "to punish some of the cowardly, racist devils" that got him fired.[127]

RUN/Hide/Fight

When McCree burst through the door, he cried, "Everyone's going to die," and pulled out a pistol. The workers ran for the exits. McCree fired 10 shots, inserted another clip, and fired again.[128]

Run/Hide/Fight/OTHER
Played dead

The first to be wounded, Lelan Brookins survived the massacre by playing dead.[129]

Case #22 – R. E. Phelon Co. Plant

Synopsis	Hastings Arthur Wise, 43, opened fire at the R.E. Phelon Company in retaliation for being fired after an argument with a supervisor.
Type of Establishment	Workplace/business
Environment	Indoors/outdoors
Motive	Revenge
Number killed	4
Number killed and injured	7
Date of murders	September 15, 1997
Weapon	9mm pistol
Location	Aiken, South Carolina
Shooter status	Executed by lethal injection in South Carolina on November 4, 2005

Overview

Hastings Arthur Wise was a 6-foot-4 ex-con who weighed more than 250 pounds. Although he had spent almost 15 years cleaning up his life, he seemed to enjoy intimidating co-workers by talking about his time in prison for breaking into a house and robbing a bank. After 4 years working at the Phelon lawnmower ignition plant, he was fired after a violent confrontation with a supervisor.[130]

Weeks later, Wise returned to the plant. He waited for the afternoon shift change to be sure that those who he thought had led to his firing, or who had gotten jobs he wanted – were there.[131] Security guard Stanley Vance saw Wise pull up in his car at the 3 p.m. shift change. Wise shot Vance in the chest, then yanked out the phone lines in the guard shack, and told the guard "I got things to do."[132]

Witnesses testified that Wise entered through a side door, went directly to the personnel office, and shot 56-year-old Charles Griffeth twice in the back. Griffeth had fired Wise two months earlier.[133] Wise began firing his pistol at everyone around, killing David Moore and Leonard Filyaw and wounding two others. Panicked workers were running to escape. Wise next found Sheryl Wood, who got a quality control job he had wanted. He shot her in the back and leg, then put a bullet in her head. After that, he fired several more shots, but no one else was killed.

Wise attempted suicide in the plant by drinking insecticide, but failed.[134] He was taken into custody by SWAT officers.

RUN/Hide/Fight

Eyewitnesses said they ran from the plant as other workers and supervisors came through shouting, "There's a man with a gun!" People were running as fast as they could, yelling "Get out! Get out!"[135]

Worker John Goad said, "I could hear the shots, and I could hear people screaming," he said."I knew I had to go...So I ran out the way I came."[136]

Run/HIDE/Fight

Two men and a woman hid under desks on the first floor, communicating with a 911 dispatcher by portable telephone.[137]

Run/Hide/Fight/OTHER
Gunman had specific targets

Wise shoved employee Carol Woody aside as he went into the Human Resources office doorway. Pam Holley was on the telephone at her desk in the outer office when Wise rushed in, searching for Charles Griffeth. The killer passed up dozens of employees during his rampage, including Zach Bush. The two looked at each other before Wise went to another area of the plant. At his trial, Wise said he didn't shoot Bush because the two had gotten along.[138]

Run/Hide/Fight/OTHER
Pled for life

When Wise returned to the outer office he found Pam Morey. "He put the gun between my eyes," she said. He then ordered her off the phone and yanked it out of the wall. "I just started pleading and praying. I said, 'I have kids. I'm a single mother. Please don't kill me,'" Mrs. Holley said. Distracted by someone who entered the building, Wise left the room. Terrified, Morey hid under her desk "because I didn't want to see somebody get shot." When she eventually heard shots farther off, she jumped up and ran from the building.[139]

Mass Shootings

Case #23 - CALTRANS MAINTENANCE YARD

Synopsis	Former Caltrans employee Arturo Reyes Torres, 41, opened fire at maintenance yard after being fired.
Type of Establishment	Workplace
Environment	Outdoors
Motive	Revenge
Number killed	4
Number killed and injured	6
Date of murders	December 19, 1997
Weapons	AK-47-type semi-automatic assault rifle; shotgun; handgun
Location	Orange, California
Shooter status	Shot and killed by police in a gun battle the same day

Overview

Arturo Torres, a former Marine, had worked for Caltrans in Orange County, California for 12 years. In mid-1997 he took $106.50 worth of highway scrap metal after being warned by a supervisor that it was against the rules. Torres was fired from his job, and unsuccessfully appealed the firing to state authorities.[140]

On December 19, 1997, Torres drove his car through the front gate of the Caltrans maintenance yard, walked out into the rain, and started firing with an AK-47 assault rifle.[141] Torres was also armed with a shotgun and a handgun.

He first went for the supervisor whom he believed unfairly targeted him for dismissal. Then he walked around a suite of trailer offices and fired, fatally wounding three men inside. The gunman had a clear view through the windows of workers as they scrambled for cover. According to police, more than 300 bullets were fired in all.[142]

Police exchanged gunfire with Reyes and chased him to a nearby intersection. Torres jumped out of his car and pulled his weapon on the driver of another car. He fired, but the driver ducked and was not hit. As the shooter went back toward his car, a gunfight with police erupted, leaving Torres dead and an officer wounded.[143]

Run/HIDE/Fight

One employee called 911 as he hid under his desk. "Help, help, there's gunfire everywhere."[144]

Case #24 – CONNECTICUT STATE LOTTERY HEADQUARTERS

Synopsis	Lottery worker Matthew Beck, 35, gunned down four bosses before committing suicide.
Type of Establishment	Workplace (State Government facility)
Environment	Indoors to outdoors
Motive	Revenge
Number killed	4
Number killed and injured	4
Date of murders	March 6, 1998
Weapon	Glock semi-automatic pistol
Location	Newington, Connecticut
Shooter status	Committed suicide by shooting himself the same day

Overview

In October of 1997, Matthew Beck, an eight-year-employee at the Connecticut State Lottery, had been granted a leave of absence for stress-related problems and was undergoing medical treatment. He had been upset about being required to perform duties that were not in his job description. When he returned to work in February, he was waiting to see if he would receive back pay. During his medical absence, a higher-paying position had been filled and he was upset that he had not received it.[145]

On March 6, 1998, Beck came to work armed with a Glock semi-automatic handgun, a butcher knife, and three clips containing at least 19 rounds each. Half an hour after reporting to work, he left his office and headed for the executive suites, where he pulled out his weapons and started shooting supervisors.[146]

Beck walked first into the office of information services chief Michael Logan. He shot Logan and stabbed him with the butcher knife. He then shot chief financial officer Linda Mlynarczyk and Rick Rubelmann, vice president of operations. Beck pointed his gun at Mylnarczyk and said, "Bye, bye," and shot her three times.[147] He also killed Rubelmann. He then chased lottery chief Otho Brown into a parking lot and shot him.

As two detectives approached Beck, he put the gun to his temple and shot himself. He died a few hours later.[148]

RUN/Hide/Fight

The sound of gunshots sent terrified workers running for the doors, where a security guard yelled for them to run for the woods nearby.[149]

RUN/Hide/Fight/OTHER
Pled for life

Lottery president Otho Brown ran from the building with Beck in pursuit. Brown stumbled in the parking lot, apparently after losing a shoe.[150] He fell to ground, raised his hands, and begged, "Don't kill me, don't kill me." Beck replied, "Aw, shut up," and shot him.[151]

Run/HIDE/Fight

About 20 workers took refuge in another part of the building used by a paint distributor.[152]

Mass Shootings

	Case #25 – WESTSIDE MIDDLE SCHOOL
Synopsis	Mitchell Scott Johnson, 13, and Andrew Douglas Golden, 11, ambushed students and teachers as they left their middle school in response to a fire alarm.
Type of Establishment	School
Environment	Outdoors
Motive	Unknown
Number killed	5
Number killed and injured	15
Date of murders	March 24, 1998
Weapons	M1 carbine .30-caliber replica carbine; .38-caliber derringer; .22-caliber derringer; two .38-caliber revolvers; two .380-caliber pistols; .357-caliber revolver; .44 magnum rifle; Remington 742 30.06-caliber rifle[153]
Location	Jonesboro, Arkansas
Shooter status	Sentenced to confinement until age 21. Johnson was released on August 11, 2005; Golden was released on May 25, 2007.

Overview

On the night of March 23, 1998, 11-year-old Andrew Douglas Golden helped his friend Mitchell Johnson, age 13, load Johnson's mother's van with weapons, snack foods, and camping supplies. The next day, Golden stole his mother's car keys and drove with Johnson to Westside Middle School, where they were students. Johnson parked the van in some nearby woods and sat on a hill in the back yard of the school. Golden went inside and pulled the fire alarm, then ran to rejoin Johnson. As students and teachers responded to what they thought was a routine fire alarm and evacuated the building, Johnson and Golden opened fire on them.[154]

The boys fired for four minutes, killing four students and a teacher, and wounding 10 more students. As police arrived on scene, Johnson and Golden ran into the woods to the van. They were caught by pursuing officers and arrested.[155]

RUN/Hide/Fight

Panicked students ran screaming back inside the school as classmates were hit by the shooters. "We thought it was just firecrackers," said one student. "I started running towards the gym."[156]

RUN/Hide/Fight/OTHER
Protected/helped

Teachers stood in front of students so that they would feel safe.[157] One teacher stepped back inside and pulled several students with her.[158]

English teacher Shannon Wright threw herself in front of sixth-grader Emma Pittman and was shot twice. Wright died in surgery, but Emma was unharmed.[159]

Case #26 – THURSTON HIGH SCHOOL

Synopsis	Thurston High School student Kipland P. Kinkel, 15, went on a shooting spree, killing his parents at home and two students at school. He was later arrested.
Type of Establishment	School
Environment	Indoors
Motive	Unknown
Number killed	4
Number killed and injured	23
Date of murders	May 21, 1998
Weapons	.22 caliber rifle; .22 caliber semi-automatic handgun; Glock semi-automatic handgun
Location	Springfield, Oregon
Shooter status	Sentenced on November 10, 1999 to 111 years in prison without the possibility of parole

Overview

On May 20, 1998, freshman Kinkel was expelled from Thurston High School for being in possession of a handgun. At about 4:00 p.m. he got his father's semi-automatic pistol, loaded it, and went to the kitchen where he shot his father in the back of the head as his father was drinking coffee. His father died instantly.[160] He then waited for his mother to get home from work. When she arrived, Kinkel told her that he loved her, then shot her repeatedly through the head and heart.[161]

On the following day, May 21, shortly before 8:00 a.m., Kinkel drove to the school, parked a few blocks away, and walked inside carrying a .22 caliber rifle, a .22 caliber handgun, and a Glock handgun. Dressed in a trench coat, he ran through the cafeteria, firing his rifle from the hip.[162] By the time the shooting ended, there were two dead and 19 wounded by gunfire. Kinkel had expended 51 rounds.[163]

RUN/HIDE/Fight

As bullets shattered the cafegteria's plate-glass windows, terrified students ran for cover and dived under tables. Student Stacy Compton said she ducked under a table; her best friend was hit in the forehead.[164]

Run/Hide/FIGHT/OTHER
Worked together to subdue gunman

Jake Ryker, 17-year-old student wrestler, was bleeding from wounds to his hand and chest. As Kinkel attempted to reload his empty weapon, Ryker tackled him. Several others quickly piled on and helped to hold the gunman until police arrived.[165]

Case #27 – COLUMBINE HIGH SCHOOL

Synopsis	Eric Harris, 18, and Dylan Klebold, 17, opened fire throughout Columbine High School before committing suicide.
Type of Establishment	School
Environment	Outdoors to indoors
Motive	Unknown
Number killed	13
Number killed and injured	37
Date of murders	April 20, 1999
Weapons	*Harris*: 12-gauge Savage Springfield 67H pump-action shotgun; 9mm carbine. *Klebold*: 9mm TEC-9 semi-automatic handgun; 12-gauge Stevens 311D double-barreled sawed-off shotgun; primarily used the Tec-9 handgun.[166] In addition, they had two 20-lb propane bombs and a pipe bomb.
Location	Littleton, Colorado
Shooter status	Both committed suicide by shooting themselves the same day

Overview

On the morning of April 29, 1999, Columbine High School seniors Eric Harris, age 18, and Dylan Klebold, age 17, arrived at the school separately and met near Harris' car. They armed two 20-pound propane bombs, setting them to explode at about 11:17 a.m., and entered the cafeteria just before the A lunch shift began. They then returned to their vehicles to wait for the bombs to explode. When that did not happen, Harris and Klebold armed themselves with their weapons, came together, and walked towards the school. At the top of the west entrance steps they threw a pipe bomb, which exploded.[167]

The two gunmen then pulled out their guns from beneath their trench coats and Harris immediately began shooting at two students who were next to the west entrance of the school. Harris removed his trench coat and shot down the West Staircase towards three youths. Harris and Klebold then turned and began shooting south in the direction of five students. Klebold walked down the steps towards the cafeteria, and Harris began to shoot down the steps at several students sitting near the cafeteria's entrance. The two youths then shot in the direction of students standing close to a soccer field, but did not hit anyone. They then made their way towards the west entrance, throwing pipe bombs as they did so, but none of them detonated.[168]

A Jefferson County deputy sheriff arrived on scene within a few minutes and began shooting at Harris and Klebold. The shooters ran inside the school and down the main north hallway, throwing pipe bombs and shooting at any individual they encountered. They proceeded to the Library hallway.[169]

At 11:29 a.m., Harris and Klebold entered the library, where a total of 52 students, two teachers and two librarians had concealed themselves. As the shooters approached the library, Harris yelled for everyone to "Get up!" When no one stood up in response, they started moving around and shooting many of those inside. While in the library, Harris and Klebold noticed police evacuating students outside the school, and then they shot out the windows of the library and in the direction of the police, who returned fire.[170]

At approximately 12:08 p.m, Harris and Klebold shouted in unison: "One! Two! Three!" These words were immediately followed by the sound of gunfire. Both had committed suicide: Harris by firing his shotgun through the roof of his mouth; Klebold by shooting himself in the left temple with his TEC-9 semi-automatic handgun.[171]

In the end, 12 students and one teacher were killed; 24 other students were injured as a direct result of the massacre. Three more were injured indirectly as they attempted to escape the school.[172]

RUN/Hide/Fight

Student Michael Johnson was hit in the face, leg and arm, yet managed to run from the scene and escaped.[173]

As Coach William David Sanders and a student walked down the Library hallway, they were confronted by both Harris and Klebold. Sanders and the student turned around and ran in the opposite direction Harris and Klebold shot at both Sanders and the student, hitting Sanders twice in the chest as he reached the South Hallway, but missing the student.

Patrick Ireland had lost and regained consciousness several times after being shot by Klebold. He managed to crawl to the library windows, where he reached out and fell into the arms of two SWAT team members standing on the roof of an emergency vehicle.[174]

RUN/Hide/Fight

Before Klebold exited the cafeteria and ascended the staircase to meet Harris, Harris severely wounded and partially paralyzed 17-year-old Anne-Marie Hochhalter as she attempted to flee.[175]

Run/**HIDE**/Fight

The student who fled with Coach Sanders ran into a classroom where he alerted the others present there to conceal themselves.[176]

Teacher Patti Nielson called emergency services as she also urged students to take cover beneath desks and remain silent. She joined Brian Anderson and three library staff in the exterior break room, into which Klebold had earlier fired shots. They locked themselves in and stayed there until they were freed, at approximately 3:30 p.m.[177]

Mass Shootings

16-year-old Kyle Velasquez had curled up underneath the computer table. Klebold shot Velasquez, hitting him in the head and back, killing him.[178]

Run/HIDE/Fight/OTHER
Gunman's decision

Harris approached a table where two girls were hiding. He bent down to look at them and dismissed them as "pathetic."[179]

In the center of the library, the killers reloaded their weapons at a table located midway across the room. Harris noticed student John Savage hiding nearby and asked him to identify himself. Savage stated his name and asked Klebold what they were doing, to which Klebold replied: "Oh, just killing people." Savage then asked if they were going to kill him. Klebold hesitated, then told Savage to leave the library He fled immediately, and escaped through the library's main entrance.[180]

Evan Todd, who had been injured in the outer room of the library, hid behind the administrative counter. When Harris and Klebold headed toward the counter, they discovered Todd. They taunted him and debated killing him, but eventually walked away. Almost immediately, 34 uninjured and 10 injured students evacuated the room through the north door, which led out to the sidewalk adjacent to the west entrance.[181]

On several occasions, the killers looked through the windows of classroom doors and made eye contact with students hiding inside, but neither shooter attempted to enter those rooms. After leaving the main office, Harris and Klebold walked towards a bathroom entrance, where they taunted students hiding inside, saying, "We know you're in there" and "Let's kill anyone we find in here." However, neither attempted to enter the bathroom.[182]

Run/Hide/Fight/OTHER
Played dead

Inside the library, 16-year-old Craig Scott hid underneath one table next to Isaiah Shoels and Matthew Keckter. Harris knelt down and shot Shoels once in the chest at close range, killing him. Klebold also knelt down and opened fire, hitting and killing Matthew Kechter. Craig Scott lay next to his friends and played dead and was uninjured.[183]

Student Mark Taylor was shot in the chest, arms and leg and fell to the ground, where he played dead and survived.[184]

Run/Hide/Fight/OTHER
Pled for life

Student Bree Pasquale had sat next to the table rather than trying to hide underneath it since there was not enough room to hide. Harris asked Pasquale if she wanted to die, and the girl responded with a plea for her life.[185]

When the two shooters approached an empty table where they again reloaded their weapons, student Valeen Schnurr, who had been badly wounded by both gunshot wounds and shrapnel, began to cry out, "Oh, God help me!" In response, Klebold approached her and asked her if she believed in God. Schnurr first replyed "no" and then "yes" in an attempt to appease Klebold. Klebold then asked her why; whereupon Schnurr replied that it was because it was what her family believed. He taunted her, reloaded his shotgun, then walked away.[186]

Run/HIDE/Fight/OTHER
Wounded while helping others

Wounded student Patrick Ireland attempted to provide first aid to another student who had been wounded in the knee. As Ireland attempted help, his head rose above the table and into Klebold's view. Klebold shot Ireland a second time, hitting him twice in the head and once in the foot. Ireland was knocked unconscious, but survived.[187]

Mass Shootings

Case #28 – Day Trading Firms

Synopsis	Day trader Mark O. Barton, 44, bludgeoned his wife and children to death, then a day later went on a shooting spree through the two day trading firms where he had made internet investments. After being cornered by police outside a gas station, he committed suicide.
Type of Establishment	Business
Environment	Indoors
Motive	Revenge
Number killed	12
Number killed and injured	21
Date of murders	July 27-29, 1999
Weapons	9mm Glock handgun; .45-caliber Colt handgun
Location	Atlanta, Georgia
Shooter status	Committed suicide by shooting himself later that day

Overview

Mark O. Barton was a day trader who had lost at least $100,000 in internet stocks and had been denied trading privileges at one day trade firm. On July 27 and 28, 1999, he bludgeoned to death his estranged wife and their two young children to "save them from a lifetime of pain."[188] On July 29, he headed to the Momentum Securities brokerage office in Atlanta, where his account had been closed after he was unable to cover his losses.[189] He exchanged pleasantries with employees and told them he wanted to make a few transactions, and said, "It's a bad trading day, and it's about to get worse." He pulled out 9mm and .45 caliber handguns, then opened fire, killing four people.[190]

Barton then walked across Piedmont Road and began shooting in the All-Tech Investment Group, a day-trading firm in the Piedmont Center building, where he killed five others.[191]

Barton escaped and shot himself to death after a five-hour manhunt when police stopped his van at a gas station.

Run/HIDE/Fight

As arriving police officers searched the Momentum offices, they found several people hiding huddled in a small room near where the victims lay. One of them had thrown a computer out the window to attract the attention of someone on the street.[192]

Run/Hide/Fight/OTHER
Gunman's decision

Four hours passed before authorities heard from someone who had seen Barton. About the same time, a woman who'd been shopping at Rich's approached her parked car. Barton walked toward her. "Don't scream or I'll shoot you," he said, according to a police report. The woman backed away. Barton told her, "Don't run or I'll shoot you." She ran, and he did not shoot.[193]

Case #29 – WEDGWOOD BAPTIST CHURCH

Synopsis	Larry Gene Ashbrook, 47, opened fire inside a church building during a teen church service before committing suicide.
Type of Establishment	Church
Environment	Indoors
Motive	Unknown (mental illness)
Number killed	7
Number killed and injured	14
Date of murders	September 15, 1999
Weapons	9mm semi-automatic handgun; .380-caliber handgun
Location	Fort Worth, Texas
Shooter status	Committed suicide by shooting himself the same day

Overview

Larry Gene Ashbrook was a loner who had great difficulty in keeping a job. His neighbors reported that he exposed himself, screamed obscenities, and kicked doors during fits of rage.[194] In September of 1999 he wrote two letters to the editor of the Fort Worth Star-Telegram complaining about the CIA, psychological warfare, assaults by co-workers, being drugged by police, and being suspected of being a serial killer, and repeated the concerns in a phone call to a local alternative newspaper. "No one will listen to me," he said. "No one will believe me."[195]

On September 15, Ashbrook entered the Wedgwood Baptist Church in Fort Worth during a service for teens and young adults. He asked one person "What's the program?" Then he shot a janitor who approached him and killed two other people before walking into the sanctuary.[196]

Cursing and shouting anti-Baptist rhetoric, Ashbrook opened fire with a with a 9mm semi-automatic handgun and a .380-caliber handgun. He reloaded several times during the shooting; three empty magazines were found at the scene. He then sat down on a back pew and shot and killed himself.[197]

Three adults and four teens were killed, and seven were wounded.

RUN/HIDE/Fight

The teens present in the sanctuary thought at first that Ashbrook's entrance and shouting was part of a skit. When he opened fire, they scrambled for cover.[198]

"We were singing a song and then in the middle of the song this guy opened the door and fired one shot," Chris Applegate said. "He just kept telling us to stay still." "We all just jumped under the benches and he fired about 10 more shots. ... Somebody said, 'Run, run,' and we all started running."[199]

Case #30 – Xerox Corp.

Synopsis	Byran Koji Uyesugi, 40, a Xerox service technician, opened fire inside the office building. He fled, and after a five-hour standoff with police, was apprehended.
Type of Establishment	Workplace
Environment	Indoors
Motive	Revenge
Number killed	7
Number killed and injured	7
Date of murders	November 2, 1999
Weapons	9mm Glock handgun
Location	Honolulu, Hawaii
Shooter status	Sentenced to life in prison without parole on August 8, 2000

Overview

Byran Koji Uyesugi began working for Xerox as a service technician in 1984. After years on the job, he was transferred to another work group. He began making accusations of harassment and product tampering about fellow repairmen. He was hostile to co-workers and alienated customers, and his work performance was below par. He had said that if he ever got fired, he would get his gun and shoot as many people as he could.[200]

Xerox management had decided to phase out the copier that Uyesugi serviced and replace it with a new machine. Uyesugi did not want to learn the new machine. On November 1, 1999, his manager notified him that he would begin training on it the next day.

On the morning of November 2, Uyesugi reported to work and went to the second floor. He opened fire with a 9mm Glock, killing his supervisor and six co-workers and firing in the direction of another co-worker who fled the building. He killed seven male employees. After the shooting, Uyesugi fled in a company van.[201]

Police closed down several streets in downtown Honolulu as they investigated the crime scene. By mid-morning, the police had Uyesugi cornered in the mountains above downtown Honolulu. After a nearly five-hour standoff, Uyesugi surrendered to police.[202]

Run/Hide/FIGHT

Jason Balatico charged toward Uyesugi in an effort to wrestle the gun away, but Uyesugi fired a "hail of shots" at him, downing him with five shots.[203]

Run/Hide/Fight/OTHER
Passed over by gunman

Lance Hamura spoke briefly to Uyesugi on the first floor before the Uyesugi embarked on his rampage on the floor above. In addition, Uyesugi walked past Ronald Yamanaka, who was having coffee in a second-floor break room, and went to a computer room at the end of the hall where two other co-workers were. He aimed the gun directly at Ron Kawamae's head, and pulled the trigger.[204]

Case #31 – Radisson Bay Harbor Hotel

Synopsis	Hotel employee Silvio Izquierdo-Leyva, 36, gunned down four co-workers at the Radisson Bay Harbor Hotel before killing a woman outside in an attempted carjacking. He was arrested shortly after the shootings.
Type of Establishment	Hotel
Environment	Indoors/outdoors
Motive	Revenge
Number killed	5
Number killed and injured	8
Date of murders	December 30, 1999
Weapons	Two handguns
Location	Tampa, Florida
Shooter status	Sentenced to life in prison without parole April 15, 2002

Overview

Cuban immigrant Silvio Izquierdo-Leyva, 36, had worked as a housekeeper at the Radisson Bay Harbor Hotel for only a few months. His sister-in-law Angela Vazquez was also employed there as housekeeping supervisor.[205]

On December 30, 1999, the hotel was crowded with football fans in town for a bowl game. On that date, Izquierdo-Leyva stormed into the lobby and opened fire at Vazquez and her daughter standing next to her, but missed. He chased Vazquez through the halls, and went outside. He pointed his gun at Rafael Barrios, the hotel's part-time bellman, who had just pulled up in his car. The gun was empty, and as Izquierdo-Leyva stopped to reload, Barrios jumped from his car and ran.

Izquierdo-Leyva went back into the hotel and started shooting again. He came back outside and fled in Barrios' car which was outside the hotel entrance. He abandoned that vehicle and pointed a handgun at a woman driving a sedan. When the woman didn't comply with his demand for the car, he shot her through the driver's side window. She quickly began to back up the car, and the gunman moved on to another car. He shot at a Jeep on the street and hit the vehicle, but the driver was able to speed away. The gunman tried for another vehicle and rejected it, then spotted a Chevy station wagon heading toward him. As the driver came to a stop, the gunman stepped up to the car, pointing his gun, and the driver surrendered it without incident.

As he drove, Izquierdo-Leyva was later surrounded by police cars a few blocks away and arrested.

Four of the five people killed were employees of the hotel.[206] The fifth victim, 56-year-old Dolores Perdomo, was the woman shot as Izquierdo-Leyva attempted to steal her car.[207]

RUN/Hide/Fight

"I heard two pops and saw people running out of the hotel," said Carson Woods. "I knew I had to get out of there."[208]

Kenny Sobaski said, "Employees from the hotel came in and said 'Get out! Get out!'" [209]

Run/HIDE/Fight

"I was in the lobby getting my paycheck when I heard shots," Diana Izquierdo said. "My mother and I hid in an office, and I saw Silvio walk by the office door." [210]

Run/Hide/Fight/OTHER
Refused to comply

The assailant tried to carjack the vehicle driven by 56-year-old Dolores Perdomo. He aimed his handgun at her, and said, "Lady, give me the car." When she didn't comply, he shot her through the driver's side window.[211]

Run/Hide/Fight/OTHER
Complied

Angel Marteliz was heading home, listening to an afternoon radio talk show. The gunman stepped from the curb as Marteliz came to a stop. He pointed his gun at Marteliz. "Take the car," Marteliz said as he stepped out. "Thank you," the gunman replied. "I knew to give him the car," Marteliz said later. "I didn't argue."[212]

Run/Hide/Fight/OTHER
Gunman's choice

Guest Robyn Gerber, a basketball team member, came face to face with the gunman as she tried to flee. "He told Robyn he wasn't interested in (shooting) anyone else, the team was OK," reported a teammate's father.[213]

Mass Shootings

Mass Shootings

Case Studies-2000s

Case #32 – Edgewater Technology Office

Synopsis	Michael McDermott, 42, opened fire on co-workers and was later arrested.
Type of Establishment	Workplace
Environment	Indoors
Motive	Revenge
Number killed	7
Number killed and injured	7
Date of murders	December 26, 2000
Weapons	AK-47-type semi-automatic rifle; 12-gauge shotgun; .32-caliber semi-automatic pistol
Location	Wakefield, Massachusetts
Shooter status	In 2002, sentenced to seven consecutive life sentences without possibility of parole

Overview

Michael "Mucko" McDermott was an application support employee for Edgewater Technology in Wakefield, Massachusetts. He had been levied by the IRS for back taxes, and his employer had been asked to garnish his wages for the tax levy.[214]

On December 26, 2000, carrying a semi-automatic rifle, a shotgun, and a pistol, McDermott entered the Edgewater office. A coworker asked, "Where are you going with that?" and he responded, "Human Resources." McDermott shot to death two employees in the reception area, then headed to the hallway, where he killed three people. When he got to the accounting office he found the door locked. After shooting out the lock with a shotgun blast, he killed two people inside the room.

McDermott then returned to the lobby, sat in a chair within reach of a black tote bag packed with ammunition and waited for the police. When police found him, he was sitting calmly and stated that he didn't speak German.[215]

Run/HIDE/Fight

The third employee in the accounting office survived by concealing herself underneath a desk. [216]

Run/Hide/Fight/OTHER
Specific targets

The District Attorney noted that the shootings appeared to have been "targeted at the individuals, rather than indiscriminate spraying of gunfire. The victims were at their work stations... The whole thing took between five and 10 minutes." [217]

Case #33 – NAVISTAR INTERNATIONAL ENGINE PLANT

Synopsis	Fired employee William D. Baker, 66, opened fire at his former workplace before committing suicide.
Type of Establishment	Workplace
Environment	Indoors
Motive	Revenge
Number killed	4
Number killed and injured	8
Date of murders	February 5, 2001
Weapons	AK-47 assault rifle
Location	DuPage County, Illinois
Shooter status	Committed suicide by shooting himself the same day

Overview

William D. Baker had been employed by Navistar as a forklift operator for nearly 40 years before being fired in 1995 for stealing engine parts. In January 2001, he was convicted in federal court of conspiracy to commit interstate theft, and was scheduled to begin a five-month prison sentence on February 6 and to pay a $195,000 fine.[218]

On the morning of February 5, Baker showed up at the Navistar plant with an arsenal of weapons in a golf bag. He approached a security guard and said that he had some "personal belongings" to give to a coworker. When the guard refused him entry and said she would have the friend come to meet him outside the building, Baker pointed a revolver at her and forced her to let him in the building.

Baker walked through the plant's diesel-engine testing room and fired at workers in his way. His actions appeared to be random and not targeting any specific individuals. He shot seven people in the engineering area, three of them fatally. After firing 25 to 30 rounds, he walked into a corner office, shot and killed his last victim, and then shot himself in the head with a handgun.[219] The rampage lasted no more than 15 minutes.

RUN/Hide/Fight

24-year-old engineer, Martin Reutimann was sitting at his desk when he heard gunfire about 10am. "I heard somebody yell, 'There's a guy in the center aisle with a gun!'" Reutimann said. Seeing people running past him, Reutimann grabbed his coat and cell phone, and desperately dialed 911.[220]

Case #34 – LOCKHEED MARTIN PLANT

Synopsis	Assembly line worker Douglas Williams, 48, opened fire at his workplace before committing suicide.
Type of Establishment	Workplace
Environment	Indoors
Motive	Rage
Number killed	5
Number killed and injured	13
Date of murders	July 3, 2003
Weapons	12-gauge shotgun; mini 14 .223 semi-automatic rifle
Location	Meridian, Mississippi
Shooter status	Committed suicide by shooting himself the same day

Overview

A factory worker, Douglas Williams, known as a "hothead" who was "mad at the world"[221] and talked about "murdering others"[222] opened fire with a shotgun at the Lockheed Martin plant where he worked. Wearing a black t-shit and camouflage pants and carrying a bandolier of ammunition, Williams entered the building with what is believed to have been two weapons, a .12 gauge shotgun and a mini 14 .223 caliber semi-automatic weapon. There were additional weapons found later in his truck. After killing five fellow employees, Williams committed suicide.

RUN/Hide/Fight

Dozens of employees ran for cover, screaming "Get out! Get out!" after Williams started firing.[223]

Assembly worker Booker Stevenson said, "...I walked to the aisle and saw him aiming his gun. I took off. Everybody took off."[224]

Mass Shootings

Case #35 – DAMAGEPLAN CONCERT

Synopsis	Nathan Gale, 25, gunned down musician Darrell "Dimebag" Abbott and three others at a *Damageplan* show before a police officer fatally shot Gale.
Type of Establishment	Concert
Environment	Indoors
Motive	Undetermined
Number killed	4
Number killed and injured	7
Date of murders	December 8, 2004
Weapons	9mm Beretta handgun
Location	Columbus, Ohio
Shooter status	Killed by police

Overview

Nathan Gale, a native of Marysville, Ohio, was a 6'5", 268-pound former Marine who had been discharged in October 2003. His mother and former employer later said that Gale told them he was discharged due to a diagnosis of paranoid schizophrenia, but he had no previous history of violence.[225]

Gale was a huge fan of the heavy metal band Damageplan, which was scheduled to perform a concert in the Alrosa Villa Club in Columbus, Ohio. By the time the band came onstage to perform shortly after 10:00 p.m., there were at least 400 people in the club.

The band was playing its opening song when Gale suddenly emerged from behind a bank of amplifiers and headed across the stage toward Dimebag. He pulled a handgun and fired three shots at close range into the back of the guitarist's head, and another that struck his hand.[226]

Fans and club employees began rushing the stage in an attempt to stop the attack; Gale turned his gun on them.

Columbus police officer James Niggemeyer had just started his shift at the precinct two miles away when the first report came of shots fired at the club. He grabbed his shotgun and entered the club through the stage door. Coming face to face with Gale, he fired and killed him.[227]

RUN/Hide/Fight

After the first shots, at 10:18 p.m., an Alrosa Villa employee fled from the club to call the police.[228]

Damageplan vocalist Patrick Lachman shouted "Call 911!" into his microphone, then jumped offstage.[229]

Run/Hide/FIGHT

Before Gale could fire again, security guard Jeff Thompson rushed at him. Thompson died after being shot twice in the body and once in the leg.[230]

Erin Halk was a member of the band's security staff. He attempted to engage the killer, and charged when Gale was reloading. He was shot and died at the scene.[231]

Other people rushed from from the wings and over the barricades onto the stage, either to help Dimebag or to try to subdue the shooter. Gale took drum tech John Brooks hostage, holding him in a headlock position after Brooks tried to wrestle the gunman to the ground.[232]

Run/Hide/Fight/OTHER
Drew attention of shooter

Fan Nathan Bray was was attempting to administer CPR to Abbott and band security chief Jeffery Thompson when he stopped, turned around and looked at Gale, with both arms out, palms up. Gale shot and killed him.[233]

Case #36 – LIVING CHURCH OF GOD

Synopsis	Church member Terry Michael Ratzmann, 44, opened fire at a church meeting at a hotel before committing suicide.
Type of Establishment	Church
Environment	Indoors
Motive	Undetermined
Number killed	7
Number killed and injured	11
Date of murders	March 12, 2005
Weapons	9mm handgun
Location	Brookfield, Wisconsin
Shooter status	Committed suicide by shooting himself the same day

Overview

Terry Michael Ratzmann was on the verge of losing his job as a computer technician, and reportedly suffered from bouts of depression and had a drinking problem. A member of the LIving Church of God in Brookfield, Wisconsin, Ratzmann was reportedly angry by a sermon which the minister had given two weeks earlier.[234]

On March 12, 2005 Ratzmann left the room in the Sheraton Hotel where the congregation held its services. He returned 20 minutes later, carrying his 9mm handgun, and walked up and down the rows of chairs, firing 22 rounds, killing the minister, the minister's son, and five others.[235]

During the shooting he reportedly spoke aloud to the congregation, telling them that he had brought 3 clips of ammunition and intended to kill the entire congregation. Midway through the second clip, Ratzmann shot and killed himself.[236]

Run/HIDE/Fight/Other

Chandra Frazier dove under a chair. "I just remember crawling on the carpet and just praying, screaming out and praying," Frazier. The man sitting in the chair was killed.[237]

Run/Hide/Fight/OTHER
Questioned gunman

One of Ratzmann's friends begged him to stop, calling him by name and saying, "Stop, stop, why?" Ratzmann did not reply, but fired a few more rounds before fatally shooting himself.[238]

Mass Shootings

Case #37 – RED LAKE HIGH SCHOOL

Synopsis	Jeffrey Weise, 16, murdered his police officer grndfather and his grandfather's girlfriend, then drove to Red Lake Senior High School on the Red Lake Indian reservation and opened fire, killing another seven people before committing suicide.
Historical Note	The Red Lake massacre was the deadliest school shooting since the Columbine killings in April 1999. [239]
Type of Establishment	School
Environment	Indoors
Motive	Unknown
Number killed	9
Number killed and injured	16
Date of murders	March 21, 2005
Weapons	9mm Glock; pump-action shotgun
Location	Red Lake, Minnesota
Shooter status	Committed suicide by shooting himself the same day

Overview

Red Lake High School student Jeffrey Weise was a loner who often wore black, and was teased by other students. His father had committed suicide, and his mother was a resident of a nursing home due to brain injuries suffered in a car accident.[240] Weise had been receiving mental health counseling and medication for depression.[241]

On the afternoon of March 21, 2005, Jeffrey Weise shot his grandfather, Daryl Lussier, with a .22 pistol while Lussier was sleeping. He is believed to have stolen Lussier's two police-issue weapons, a 9 mm Glock and a pump-action shotgun. Weise shot Michele Sigana, Lussier's girlfriend and police partner, when she returned home.[242]

Mass Shootings

Weise then drove a patrol vehicle (believed to be his grandfather's) to the high school building. Passing through the building's main entrance, he encountered unarmed security guard Derrick Brun, who was manning the school's metal detector. Weise fatally shot Brun, and then continued to fire, killing five students and a teacher and injuring seven others.[243]

When police officers arrived, they exchanged gunfire with Weise, who then apparently retreated to a classroom and killed himself. The entire episode lasted about 10 minutes.[244] All of the dead students, including the killer, were found in one room.[245]

Run/HIDE/Fight

During the shootings, teachers led students from one room to another in an effort to move away from the sound of the shooting.[246]

One quick-thinking teacher locked the classroom door and thwarted Weise's attempt to enter.[247]

Run/Hide/Fight/OTHER
Played dead

15-year-old Lance Crowe survived by playing dead, lying among those killed. From the floor, Crowe watched as the shooter came back into the classroom and killed himself just a few feet away as the police closed in.[248]

Case #38 – Mail Processing Center

Synopsis	Former postal worker Jennifer Sanmarco, 44, shot dead a former neighbor, then drove to the mail processing plant where she had worked and opened fire, killing six employees before committing suicide.
Type of Establishment	Post Office
Environment	Indoors
Motive	Revenge
Number killed	7
Number killed and injured	7
Date of murders	January 30, 2006
Weapons	15-round 9mm pistol
Location	Goleta, California
Shooter status	Committed suicide by shooting herself the same day

Overview

Jennifer Sanmarco had a history of bizarre behavior, according to those who knew her. She She carried on conversations with herself and rummaged through dumpsters. She had made racist comments to coworkers, and in 2004 expressed the intent to start a publication called "The Racist Press." She was a loner with no known family or friends.[249]

Sanmarco's mental problems were the apparent reason for her retirement on medical leave after six years of employment at the mail processing center in Goleta, California.[250]

On January 30, 2006, Sanmarco shot and killed her former neighbor, Beverly Graham, and then drove to her former place of employment, the mail processing plant, about 9:00 p.m. She drove through a gate behind another car, then took an employee's identification badge at gunpoint. She shot two people in the parking lot before entering the building and shooting four more. She then took her own life.[251]

Authorities said it was unclear whether Sanmarco targeted specific employees at the postal center, but a postal inspector said "chances are" she knew the people she was shooting at.[252]

RUN/Hide/Fight

About 80 of the approximately 300 people who work at the mail-sorting center were on hand when Sanmarco arrived. Authorities said that many of them fled to a fire station across the street when the shooting began.[253]

Run/Hide/Fight/OTHER
Complied

San Marco gained entry to the building by taking an employee's identification badge at gunpoint. That worker was not hurt.[254]

Case #39 – RAVE AFTER-PARTY

Synopsis	Kyle Aaron Huff, 28, opened fire at a rave after-party in the Capitol Hill neighborhood of Seattle before committing suicide.
Type of Establishment	Residence
Environment	Outdoors to indoors
Motive	Unknown
Number killed	6
Number killed and injured	8
Date of murders	March 25, 2006
Weapons	12-gauge Winchester shotgun; 40-caliber semi-automatic Ruger handgun
Location	Seattle, Washington
Shooter status	Committed suicide by shooting himself the same day

Overview

Kyle Aaron Huff was a former pizza delivery man and an art student who was one of the first to arrive at an 'after-party' following a rave in Seattle, Washington. The early-morning party was held in a bungalow in a quiet residential area called Capitol Hill. Huff kept to himself, was quiet and polite, and made friendly small talk with others present.[255]

Close to 7 a.m., Huff left the house and went to his truck parked nearby. He retrieved a 12-gauge pistol-grip Winchester Defender shotgun and a .40-caliber semi-automatic Ruger handgun, over 300 rounds worth of ammunition, and a can of spray paint.[256]

Huff spray-painted the word "NOW" on the sidewalk and on the steps of a neighboring home, then pulled out the handgun. He walked up to a landing near the front porch of the party house and opened fire.[257] Huff fired repeatedly as he proceeded through the house, killing four men and two women.

Officer Steve Leonard, patrolling in the neighborhood, heard shots fired and went to the scene. When [Huff] emerged carrying a shotgun, Leonard ordered him to put down the weapon. Huff turned the gun on himself and fired a fatal shot.[258] The shooting inside the house had lasted only minutes.

RUN/Hide/Fight

People fled the house, some through the back door and others out the windows. A neighbor living across the street heard six shots, looked out his window, and saw people scattering from the home.[259]

Run/HIDE/Fight

"He randomly came up, fired, and people scrambled to find a hiding place," said one of those inside the house.[260]

Alissa Dunn and Gary Will were in an upstairs bathroom. When they heard the shots, they locked the door and hid in the bathtub. Huff fired a round through the door, missing the couple crouching in the tub.[261]

One person hid under a bed and saw the shooter's feet as he walked into the room. He heard Huff say, "I've got enough ammunition to shoot everybody."[262]

A 911 dispatcher asked a female caller if the shooter was still there. "I don't know," a hushed, frightened voice says. "We're hiding."[263]

Huff also went down into the basement, where three men were hiding.[264]

Run/Hide/Fight/OTHER
Bystander Responses

At least one of the 911 calls came from inside the house. Other calls were made by neighbors. Neighbor Albert Sbragia heard the shots and looked out his bedroom window. He saw Huff firing at the front of the house. His wife Dawn called 911, and told her children to lay down on the floor. Across the street, William Lowe was just getting up. He heard shots and called 911.

Mass Shootings

Cesar Clemente woke up to the sound of gunshots. After calling 911, he went to his door and saw two injured people fleeing into bushes. "You guys come over here," he said. One man, shot in the arm and side, made it across the street and into Clemente's home. The other person collapsed in the bushes.[265]

Mass Shootings

Case #40 – NICKEL MINES AMISH SCHOOL

Synopsis	Charles Carl Roberts, 32, shot 10 young girls in a one-room Amish schoolhouse, killing 5, before taking his own life.
Type of Establishment	School
Environment	Indoors
Motive	Unknown
Number killed	5
Number killed and injured	10
Date of murders	October 2, 2006
Weapons	9mm semi-automatic pistol; 12-gauge shotgun; rifle
Location	Bart Township, Pennsylvania
Shooter status	Committed suicide by shooting himself the same day

Overview

Charles Carl Roberts was a milk tank truck driver who lived in the town of Bart in Lancaster County, Pennsylvania. On October 2, 2006, he armed himself with a 9mm semi-automatic pistol, a 12-gauge shotgun and a rifle, along with a bag of some 600 rounds of ammunition, two cans of smokeless powder, two knives, and a stun gun, along with rolls of tape, some tools, and a change of clothes.[266]

Roberts drove to the West Nickel Mines School, a one-room Amish schoolhouse, and entered at just before 10:00 a.m. He sent the boys and adults outside, then barricaded the doors with lumber nailed into place. He bound the girls' feet with wire and plastic ties and lined them up along the chalkboard, then opened fire.[267]

Roberts had called his wife from a cell phone shortly before the shooting began, saying he was "acting out in revenge for something that happened 20 years ago." Once police were able to enter the school, they found Roberts dead of a self-inflicted gunshot wound.[268]

Roberts appeared to have no grudge against the Amish community, and may have picked the school because it was nearby and had little or no security.[269]

RUN/Hide/Fight/Other

Nine-year-old Emma Fisher escaped in the beginning; her two older sisters stayed inside.[270]

Run/Hide/Fight/OTHER
Gunman's decision

Initially the gunman released all 15 male students present, along with a pregnant woman and three parents with infants.[271]

Run/Hide/Fight/OTHER
Pled for life

The oldest girl, 13-year-old Marian Fisher, appealed to Roberts to shoot her first, apparently in an effort to spare the younger girls, according to her younger sister Barbie who survived. Barbie appealed to Roberts to shoot her next. She received 9mm bullet wounds in the hand, leg, and shoulder but survived.[272]

Case #41 – Trolley Square Mall

Synopsis	Sulejman Talović, 18, rampaged through a shopping center until he was shot dead by pollice.
Type of Establishment	Shopping mall
Environment	Indoors
Motive	Unknown
Number killed	5
Number killed and injured	9
Date of murders	February 12, 2007
Weapon	Shotgun; .38 caliber pistol
Location	Salt Lake City, Utah
Shooter status	Shot dead by police the same day

Overview

Bosnian immigrant Sulejman Talović, 18, lived in Salt Lake City with his mother. He was enrolled in several city schools before withdrawing in 2004. Neighbors rarely saw him and he was considered a loner.[273]

On February 12, 2007, Talović took a backpack full of ammunition, a shotgun, and a .38 caliber pistol, and went to the Trolley Square shopping mall in Salt Lake City. Stepping out of his car, he immediately began shooting, firing at anyone in his line of sight.[274] He killed two people, then a third as he came through a door. Five others were shot inside a gift shop.[275]

Kenneth Hammnond, an off-duty police officer, was at the mall for dinner with his wife. When he realized what was happening, he drew his gun and told his wife to call the police. He fired on Talović, drawing the gunman's attention until other officers could arrive. "I've been in situations before where I've had to chase a guy who was pointing a gun at me," Hammond said, "I feel like I was there and did what I had to do."[276]

After Talović was cornered and shooting at officers, an active shooter contact team comprised of Salt Lake City Police Department SWAT team members arrived and shot him.[277]

Run/HIDE/Fight

Marie Smith, a store manager, said she had seen the gunman through the store window. "He didn't seem upset, or like he was on a rampage," sahe said. She cralwed to an employee restroom to hide with others.[278]

Matt Lund was visiting his wife who was manager of the Secret Garden children's clothing store, when he heard the first shots. The couple and three others hid in a storage room for about 40 minutes, still able to hear the violence.[279]

Barb McKeown, 60, was in an antiques shop when two frantic women ran in and reported gunshots. "Then we heard shot after shot after shot..," said McKeown. She and three others hid under a staircase until it was safe to leave.[280]

For hours after the rampage had ended, police searched stores for frightened shoppers and employees who were still in hiding, waiting for safe escort from the scene.[281]

Run/Hide/Fight/OTHER
Warned others

One of the wounded shoppers, Shawn Munns, was alone outside the mall after a meal with his wife and two stepchildren when Talovic blasted him with a shotgun. With dozens of pellets embedded in his side, Munns staggered into the nearby Hard Rock Café and warned diners about the gunman, and told them to lock the doors.[282]

Case #42 – VIRGINIA TECH UNIVERSITY

Synopsis	Virginia Tech student Seung-Hui Cho, 29, opened fire on his school's campus before committing suicide.
Historical note	The Virginia Tech massacre was the deadliest mass shooting in modern U.S. history
Type of Establishment	University campus
Environment	Indoors
Motive	Unknown (mental illness)
Number killed	32
Number killed and injured	61
Date of murders	April 16, 2007
Weapons	.22-caliber Walther P22 semi-automatic pistol; 9mm Glock 19 semi-automatic pistol
Location	Blacksburg, Virginia
Shooter status	Committed suicide by shooting himself the same day

Overview

Seung-Hui Cho was a South Korean who had moved to the U.S. at eight years of age. In 2007 he was a senior majoring in English at Virginia Tech. In middle school he was diagnosed with a severe anxiety disorder as well as major depressive disorder. He received therapy and treatment until his junior year of high school.[283] At Virginia Tech, he had a history of incidents including allegations of stalking, referrals to counseling, and several of his writings caused concern among classmates and teachers.[284]

At about 7:15 a.m. in West Ambler Johnston Hall, a dorm, Cho shot and killed two students. He returned to his room and re-armed himself, and mailed a package containing pictures, digital files and documents to NBC News.[i] At close to 10:00 a.m., police responded to a 911 call reporting that shots had been fired at Norris Hall, a building about a half-mile away on the opposite side of the campus. They found that the building's front doors had been chained from the inside, so that no one could exit and police could not enter.[285]

Cho entered classroom after classroom and shot people at random. He killed 25 students and five faculty members, and wounded 29 in Norris Hall, where police reports indicate that Cho fired about 170 rounds. Officers forced their way into the building and followed the sound of gunshots to the second floor. As police began closing in on Cho, he shot and killed himself.[286]

RUN/Hide/Fight/Other

As Cho proceeded through Norris Hall shooting, students leapt to safety from the windows of their classrooms.[287]

Run/HIDE/Fight

Hearing the commotion on the floor below, Kevin Granata and Wally Grant brought 20 students from a nearby classroom into an office where the door could be locked.[288]

Run/Hide/FIGHT

Air Force ROTC student Matthew LaPorte is reported to have attempted to tackle Cho from behind, but was fatally injured in the attempt.[289]

Run/Hide/Fight/OTHER
Tried to help others

Several people tried to help others during the attack. Around 9:30 am, a student walked into Room 211 at Norris Hall and alerted the occupants that a shooting had occurred at West Ambler Johnston.[290]

---

[i] In the media package sent to NBC, Cho discussed "martyrs like Eric and Dylan," apparently referring to the Columbine High School gunmen. The Virginia Tech massacure occurred just four days before the eight-year-anniversary of the Columbine shooting.

Run/Hide/Fight/OTHER
Barricaded doors

Professor Liviu Librescu held the door of his classroom shut while Cho attempted to enter the room. He was able to keep Cho out until the students had escaped through the windows. The professor was eventually shot five times and killed. Professor Couture-Nowak looked Cho in the eye in the hallway. She ordered her students to the back of the classroom for their safety and made a fatal attempt to barricade the door.[291]

Around 9:40 a.m., students in Norris 205 heard gunshots. The students barricaded the door with a large table, while Cho shot several times through the door. No one in that classroom was killed.[292]

Run/Hide/Fight/OTHER
Drew attention of shooter

Waleed Shaalan, a teaching assistant and student from Egypt, although wounded, distracted Cho from a nearby student after the shooter had returned to the room. Shaalan was shot a second time and died.[293]

Partahi Mamora Halomoan Lumbantoruan protected fellow student Guillermo Colman by diving on top of him. Multiple gunshots killed Lumbantoruan, but Colman was protected by Lumbantoruan's body.[294]

Several students barricaded the door of Room 207 after the first attack and helped the wounded. Cho returned minutes later, but students Derek O'Dell and Katelyn Carney prevented him from re-entering; both were injured.[295]

Run/Hide/Fight/OTHER
Left hiding place

Kevin Granata and Wally Grant left the locked room and went downstairs to investigate. Both were shot by Cho. Grant was wounded and survived, but Granata died from his injuries. None of the students locked in Granata's office were injured.[296]

Mass Shootings

Mass Shootings

Case #43 – Apartment Building

Synopsis	Off-duty sheriff's deputy Tyler Peterson, 20, opened fire inside an apartment where his ex-girlfriend and friends were gathered for a movie-watching party, killing six and wounding another. He fled the scene and later committed suicide.
Type of Establishment	Residence
Environment	Indoors
Motive	Domestic dispute
Number killed	6
Number killed and injured	7
Date of murders	October 7, 2007
Weapons	AR-15 rifle; pistol
Location	Crandon, Wisconsin
Shooter status	Committed suicide by shooting himself the same day

Overview

Tyler Peterson had just been hired as a deputy in the Forest County Sheriff's Department, and was a part-time officer at the Crandon Police Department in Crandon, Wisconsin.

At about 2:30 a.m. on the morning of October 7, 2007, he entered an apartment complex where a group of friends ages 14 to 20 had been eating pizza and watching movies. One of those present was Peterson's ex-girlfriend, Jordanne Murray, with whom Peterson engaged in a loud argument. She demanded that Peterson leave.[297]

Peterson went to his truck, got his police-issued AR-15 rifle, went back to the party and opened fire. He killed six of those present.[298]

The first officer who responded to the shooting was shot at, but his wounds were superficial from glass fragments. Peterson drove away and went to the house of some friends, where he confessed what he

Mass Shootings

had done. His friends were unable to convince him to turn himself in. He left without harming them.[299]

Authorities were able to establish contact with Peterson and talked with him about surrendering. He went into some nearby woods with his pistol, where he committed suicide with a gunshot to the head.

Run/Hide/Fight/OTHER
Played dead

One of the partygoers survived because he played dead after being shot three times.[300]

Case #44 – WESTROADS MALL

Synopsis	Robert A. Hawkins, 19, opened fire inside a mall before committing suicide.
Type of Establishment	Department store
Environment	Indoors
Motive	Uncertain
Number killed	8
Number killed and injured	13
Date of murders	December 5, 2007
Weapon	AK-47 semi-automatic rifle
Location	Omaha, Nebraska
Shooter status	Committed suicide by shooting himself the same day

Overview

Robert A. Hawkins had been fired from his job at McDonald's, and had recently broken up with his girlfriend. He had a felony drug conviction and several misdemeanor cases filed against him, including having been arrested in November of 2007 for being a minor in possession of alcohol. He was scheduled to appear in court in December.[301]

On December 5, Hawkins took an AK-47 7.62x39mm semi-automatic rifle, apparently stolen from his stepfather's house, along with two 30-round magazines, concealed in a sweatshirt, into a Nebraska department store, took the elevator up to the third floor, and opened fire on customers and store employees. He killed eight people and wounded five, then turned the gun on himself and killed himself. Hawkins left a suicide note that said, in part, that he was sorry for everything and did not want to be a burden any longer, that he was worthless, and "Now I'll be famous."[302]

RUN/Hide/Fight

Witness Shawn Vidlak said the shots sounded like a nail gun, and thought it was noise from construction work. "People started screaming about gunshots," Vidlak said. "I grabbed my wife and kids. We got out of there as fast as we could." [303]

Witnesses described chaos and shoppers frantically running away from the Von Maur store, where the shooting began just before 2 p.m. [304]

Run/HIDE/Fight

Some shoppers and mall employees ran to hide in clothes racks, dressing rooms, and bathrooms after hearing the shots. [305]

Kristy Wright realized what was happening and yelled "There's a shooter." She tried to turn and run; her friend was frozen in fear. They went to a nearby store, told the employees what had happened and asked if they could hide there. A manager led Wright and others to a room in the back of the store." [306]

"I saw employees taking a bunch of people into the dressing room, but I didn't want to go," shopper Jennifer Kramer said, "I didn't know if this guy was going to come looking for people in dressing rooms, so we hid in a pants rack towards the back of the men's department." [307]

Von Maur employee Keith Fidler said he huddled in the corner of the men's clothing department with about a dozen other employees until police yelled to get out of the store. Another employee who worked in the store's third-floor service department heard shots and went with coworkers and customers into a back closet, emerging about a half-hour later when police shouted to come out with their hands up. [308]

Case #45 – City Council Meeting

Synopsis	Charles Lee Thornton, 52, went on a rampage at city hall before being shot and killed by police.
Type of Establishment	Government facility
Environment	Outdoors to indoors
Motive	Revenge
Number killed	5
Number killed and injured	7
Date of murders	February 7, 2008
Weapons	.44 magnum revolver; 40-caliber handgun
Location	Kirkwood, Missouri
Shooter status	Killed during a shootout with police the same day

Overview

Charles Lee Thornton was a lifelong resident of Meacham Park, which had long been an unincorporated section of St. Louis County, Missouri. In 1992 commercial development was planned for the community; Thornton received some of the development work for his construction company, but was apparently resentful that he did not receive as much as he wanted. In 1999 he filed a complaint with the Equal Employment Opportunity Commission alleging racial discrimination in the awarding of contracts.[309]

Beginning in 1996 Thornton began receiving citations for various code violations. By May 2002, he had received more than 150 tickets, and had been ordered to pay nearly $20,000 in fines and court costs. He filed for bankruptcy in December 1999 but failed to comply with his repayment plan; he also never paid any of the code violation fines. He regularly appeared at city council meetings complaining of persecution, fraud and coverup by city officials.[310]

Mass Shootings

On May 13, 2002, Thornton was convicted of assault on the city's public works director.[ii] He was also arrested and handcuffed at two city council meetings in 2006, charged with disorderly conduct. There were other instances of misdemeanor charges and public misconduct in subsequent years.

On February 7, 2008, Thornton was armed with a revolver and went to city hall where the City Council was meeting. He shot and killed police officer Sgt. William Biggs, who was walking across the street, then took the officer's .40 caliber handgun and entered city hall. Reaching Council chambers, he shot police officer Tom Ballman in the head, then moved on to shoot at close range the public works director, two council members, the mayor, and a reporter. In total, the gunman killed five and wounded two others.[311]

The gunfire was audible to the police department across the street, and two officers rushed to council chambers. Thornton fired on them from behind a desk; they returned fire and Thornton was killed.[312]

RUN/Hide/Fight

In council chambers Thornton chased City Attorney John Hessel, who slowed the gunman by throwing chairs at him until Hessel could escape.[313]

[ii] Yost became one of Thornton's murder victims.

Case #46 – NORTHERN ILLINOIS UNIVERSITY

Synopsis	Steven Kazmierczak, 28, opened fire in a university lecture hall, then shot and killed himself before police arrived.
Type of Establishment	University
Environment	Indoors
Motive	Unknown
Number killed	5
Number killed and injured	23
Date of murders	February 14, 2008
Weapons	Remington 870 shotgun; 9mm Glock handgun; 9mm Sig Sauer handgun; .380 Hi-Point handgun
Location	DeKalb, Illinois
Shooter status	Committed suicide by shooting himself the same day

Overview

Steven Kazmierczak was a former student at Northern Illinois University (NIU) who "...had a very good academic record, no record of trouble" according to NIU President John G. Peters.[314] While at NIU, he wrote a paper called "No Crazies With Guns," in which he used the April 2007 Virginia Tech massacre to analyze whether mentally ill people should have access to guns. Kazmierczak had a history of attempted suicides and was hospitalized nine times for psychiatric issues before 2001.[315]

He was discharged from the U.S. Army before completion of basic training for lying about his mental illness. In 2008, according to Kazmierczak's girlfriend, he had been taking Xanax (an anti-anxiety medication), Ambien (a sleep aid), and Prozac (an antidepressant), all prescribed by a psychiatrist.[316] In early 2008, Kazmierczak's behavior seemed to be more erratic.

At approximately 3:00 p.m. on February 14, 2008, Kazmierczak, carrying a guitar case, entered a large lecture hall in Cole Hall on the campus of NIU. The hall contained 150 to 200 students in an oceanography class. The door Kzamierczak used led directly to the stage in front of the room. He removed a Remington 870 shotgun from the guitar case, and three handguns from under his coat, and began firing into the crowd of students. Five students were killed and 18 were wounded.[317]

John Giovanni, 20, and others said the gunman aimed at the center of the auditorium. "He just fires right into the audience," Giovanni said. "He didn't say a word. It didn't look like he was aiming directly at someone. I think he was trying to hit as many people as he could."[318]

Doug Quesnel, 22, said "Nothing seemed...wrong until the shots went off."[319]

RUN/Hide/Fight

Harold Ng, 21, said the danger didn't register even after the firing began. It wasn't until the other students in the class began to run in a panic that Ng began to run. While running, he was shot in the back of the head. "I just swiped the back of my head with my hand, and then when I looked at my hand it was all bloody," Ng said. He ran to a nearby hall.[320]

When the shooting began, chaos erupted. Students dropped to the floor and began crawling, running, and shoving their way to the auditorium doors.[321]

John Giovanni crouched down and bolted for the doors, thinking to himself that a moving target would be more difficult to hit. "I was pushing through people," he said. "You need to get out. You never know how good of a marksman he is. . . . My goal was getting out there and running as far as I could to be safe."[322]

Senior Desiree Smith said, "I dropped to the ground under my seat, and could see another girl down there. We just stared at each other. I grabbed her leg and was squeezing it for about five seconds. Then we moved all of a sudden. Everyone was army-crawling toward the back of the auditorium on the floor. As soon as I reached the door, I got halfway hunched over, and then started to run as soon as I got outside.[323]

Freshman Jillian Martinez said, "I ran out of there as fast as I could..Everyone started rushing for doors. Everybody fell over everybody."[324]

NIU Police Chief Donald Grady said students were running through any door they could find in order to get out.[325]

Run/HIDE/Fight

Students who didn't run attempted to hide under their seats or under desks, according to freshman Loren Weese, 18, who was seated on the aisle about halfway up the auditorium. "A lot of people fell," she said. "I don't know if they did that on purpose to avoid being shot."[326]

Run/Hide/Fight/OTHER
Ducked

Class instructor Joseph Peterson was standing on a stage at the front of the auditorium when the gunman burst in and started shooting. Peterson ducked and was shot in the arm.[327]

Mass Shootings

Case #47 – Pinelake Health & Rehab Center

Synopsis	Robert Stewart, 45, opened fire at a nursing home where his estranged wife worked, before he was shot and arrested by a police officer.
Type of Establishment	Nursing home
Environment	Outdoors to indoors
Motive	Domestic
Number killed	8
Number killed and injured	10
Date of murders	March 29, 2009
Weapons	Handgun; shotgun; .22 caliber rifle
Location	Carthage, North Carolina
Shooter status	Sentenced to 142 years-to-179-1/2 years in prison on September 2, 2011

Overview

Robert Stewart and his wife had a rocky relationship that extended over many years. They married as teens and divorced three years later. Both were involved in other marriages before they reunited and married a second time in June 2002, then separated again. Not long after the last split, Stewart's wife was working as a nursing assistant at the Pinelake Helath and Rehab center, a 110-bed nursing home and care center for patients with Alzheimer's disease.[328]

On March 29, 2009, Stewart, armed with weapons described by one witness as a "deer gun and a shotgun" and dressed in a bib overall, pulled into the parking lot of the nursing home just before 10:00 a.m., where he shot several times at his wife's car, shattering its windows. He also shot at Michael Lee Cotten, there to visit a great-aunt, in his car, when he pulled into the parking lot, shattering the car windows and hitting Cotten with a pellet in the left shoulder.[329]

Stewart entered the facility and went down the hall apparently searching for his wife, who had been reassigned to the Alzheimer unit that morning. Upon realizing that his wife wasn't where she usually worked, he headed to the area for Alzheimer's patients which was secured by passcode-protected doors. As he proceeded through the halls, Stewart fired at residents in their beds or wheelchairs.[330]

Police received the first emergency calls at approximately 10:00 a.m. and the only police officer on duty, Justin Garner, was dispatched to the scene about one minute later. At about 10:05 a.m., Officer Garner entered the building alone and confronted Stewart. After refusing several orders to drop his weapon, Stewart lowered his shotgun and fired a shot at Garner, wounding him three times in the leg. Garner returned fire and hit the gunman in the upper chest and was able to take him into custody.[331]

Run/HIDE/Fight

Stewart's wife survived the shooting unharmed, hiding in a bathroom in the Alzheimer's ward secured by passcode-protected doors.[332]

After being shot, Michael Cotton ran into the building and warned those inside about the gunman. He ran to his aunt's room. When he heard the gunman enter the building, he hid in a bathroom. "You could hear him coming down the hallway and just shooting randomly, and people hollering and screaming," he said.[333]

RUN/Hide/Fight/OTHER
Tried to protect others

Nurse Jerry Avant was trying to get patients to safety. Stewart cornered the nurse in a hallway and shot him at least two times. Avant later died in surgery.[334]

Case #48 – AMERICAN CIVIC ASSOCIATION CENTER

Synopsis	Jiverly Wong,[iii] 41, opened fire at a center for immigrants before committing suicide.
Type of Establishment	Public building
Environment	Indoors
Motive	Revenge
Number killed	13
Number killed and injured	17
Date of murders	April 3, 2009
Weapons	9mm Beretta; .45-caliber Beretta
Location	Binghamton, New York
Shooter status	Committed suicide by shooting himself the same day

Overview

Jiverly Wong came to the United States from Vietnam with his family when he was young. Even after years in this country, he "felt degraded because of his inability to speak English, and he was upset about that."[335] He was also upset about recently losing a job when the assembly plant where he worked was closed. He was described as an "angry loner who loved guns." A former co-worker used to joke with a friend about how they thought Wong would "come in mad one day and shoot people. He seemed like that kind of guy."[336]

Wong had been taking English classes at the American Civic Association in Binghamton, New York, which helps refugees and immigrants, until dropping out in March of 2009. On April 3 at about 10:30 a.m., Wong barricaded the rear door of the Civic Association with a vehicle and entered the building. He then opened fire on the people inside.[337] Two of the Civic association's receptionists were among the first victims.[338]

[iii] Recently changed his name to Voong

The area where the violence was then focused was a classroom, just off the main reception areas, where an ESL class was being given to students. Everyone who was in that classroom suffered a gunshot wound. Wong entered and began executing victims, taking some hostage. Police arrived within minutes of the 911 calls; it was later revealed, that when Wong heard the sirens, he took his own life by turning one of his guns against himself. In all, Wong fired 99 rounds; 88 from a 9 mm Beretta and 11 from a .45-caliber Beretta.[339]

RUN/HIDE/Fight

Some of those present managed to escape to a basement, while more than a dozen hid in a closet.[340]

Run/HIDE/Fight/OTHER
Played dead

Receptionist Shirley DeLucia was one of the first to be shot, being hit in the stomach. She then pretended to be dead and, when the gunman moved on, hid under a desk and called 911. She stayed on the line for 39 minutes and relayed information until she was rescued.[341]

Run/Hide/Fight/OTHER
Protected others

Vietnamese immigrant Long Huynh attempted to shield his wife. "I pushed her to the ground and covered her with my body," he said. One bullet passed through him and killed his wife.[342]

Case #49 – Fort Hood Army Base

Synopsis	Army psychiatrist Nidal Malik Hasan, 39, opened fire on an Army base. Hasan was injured during the attack and later arrested.
Historical note	The Fort Hood attack was the worst terrorist attack on U.S. soil since the 9/11 attack.
Type of Establishment	U.S. Army base
Environment	Indoors
Motive	Terrorism
Number killed	13
Number killed and injured	45
Date of murders	November 5, 2009
Weapons	FN Five-seven semi-automatic pistol; .357 magnum revolver
Location	Fort Hood, Texas
Shooter status	In jail awaiting trial

Overview

Nidal Malik Hasan was born in Virginia to parents who had emigrated from Jordan to the U.S. Hasan joined the U.S. Army, rose to the rank of Major, and worked as a psychiatrist stationed at Ft. Hood in Texas. He worked at the Soldier Readiness Center, where personnel receive routine treatment immediately prior to and returning from deployment.

A Muslim, Hasan reported to family that he felt that as a Muslim committed to his prayers he was discriminated against and not treated with the respect due an officer.[343] He was also distressed over his planned deployment to the Middle East, especially after counseling soldiers who had returned from there suffering post-traumatic stress disorder.

Mass Shootings

At least six months before November 2009, Hasan had come to the attention of federal authorities due to Internet postings he had apparently made discussing suicide bombings and other threats. He had also been vocal about his concern that the U.S. war on terrorism was a war against Islam.[344]

In the early afternoon of November 5, 2009, Hasan entered The Soldier Readiness Center. According to eyewitnesses, he sat at an empty table, bowed his head for several seconds, then stood up and shouted "*Allahu Akbar!*" before opening fire on defenseless soldiers sitting in a waiting area, then hunting down wounded soldiers in an attempt to finish them off. Many of the wounded soldiers were shot multiple times while they lay on the floor.[345]

Base civilian police Sergeant Kimberly Munley arrived on the scene in response to the report of an emergency at the center. She encountered Hasan leaving the building as he pursued a wounded soldier. Munley and Hasan exchanged gunfire; Munley was hit three times, in the leg and in the wrist, and fell to the ground. In the meantime, civilian police officer Sergeant Mark Todd arrived and fired at the gunman. Hasan was finally felled by shots from Todd and Munley. Todd approached the gunman and kicked a pistol out of his hand. Hasan was placed in handcuffs as he fell unconscious. The incident lasted about 10 minutes.[346]

In a 2011 special report, the Homeland Security and Government Affairs Committee charged that the FBI should have recognized that Hasan had become an adherent of "violent Islamist extremism" before he went on the rampage.[347]

As of publication of this book, Hasan is awaiting trial. He attempted to plead guilty to 13 counts of premeditated murder, but Army rules prohibit a judge from accepting a guilty plea to charges carrying the death penalty.

RUN/HIDE/Fight

Civilian police officr Sgt. Mark Todd stated that Hasan was firing at people as they were trying to run and hide.[348]

Run/Hide/FIGHT

Unarmed Army Reserve Capt. John Gaffaney tried to stop Hasan, but was mortally wounded in the process.[349]

Witnesses reported that civilian physician assistant Michael Cahill tried to charge Hasan with a chair before being shot and killed.[350]

Run/Hide/Fight/OTHER
Helped others

As the shooting continued outside, nurses and medics entered the building, secured the doors with a belt, and began helping the wounded.[351]

Mass Shootings

Mass Shootings

Case Studies - 2010s

Case #50 - HARTFORD BEER DISTRIBUTORSHIP

Synopsis	Omar S. Thornton, 34, shot up his workplace after facing disciplinary issues, then committed suicide.
Type of Establishment	Workplace
Environment	Indoors
Motive	Revenge
Number killed	8
Number killed and injured	10
Date of murders	August 3, 2010
Weapons	15-shot Ruger SR9 pistol
Location	Manchester, Connecticut
Shooter status	Committed suicide by shooting himself the same day

Overview

Omar S. Thornton worked for the Harford Distributors in Manchester, Connecticut. Thornton, who was black, told his girlfriend that he had problems with coworkers who were racist, and that his grievances were not addressed.

Thornton had been recorded on surveillance video in the warehouse stealing beer. On August 3, 2010, he was called in to a disciplinary hearing, and was given the options of being fired or of resigning. He did not argue or protest, but agreed to resign. Then he pulled a Ruger SR9 handgun from what appeared to be a lunchbag, and began firing as he ran through the warehouse.[352] Within moments, he had killed eight workers, and seriously injured two others.

Mass Shootings

Police responded and began clearing the building. In a final phone call to his mother, Thornton told her he had shot "the five racists." Shortly afterward, he put the gun to his head and killed himself.[353]

Case #51 - Rep. Gabrielle Giffords Public Meeting

Synopsis	Jared Loughner, 22, opened fire outside a grocery store during a constituent meeting with U.S. Representative Gabrielle Giffords before he was subdued by bystanders and arrested.
Type of Establishment	Shopping center parking loat
Environment	Outdoors
Motive	Political
Number killed	6
Number killed and injured	21
Date of murders	January 8, 2011
Weapon	9mm Glock 19 semi-automatic pisol
Location	Tucson, Arizona
Shooter status	On November 8, 2012, sentenced to serve seven consecutive life terms plus 140 years in prison, without parole

Overview

Jared Lee Loughner dropped out of high school in 2006. He was fired from his job at a Quiznos restaurant, with his manager saying he had undergone a personality transformation. After this, Loughner briefly volunteered at a local animal shelter, walking dogs, but he was asked not to return due to a "failure to follow instructions."

A close friend reported that after Loughner's girlfriend broke up with him, he began to use marijuana and other drugs. He attempted to enlist in the U.S. Army, but was rejected as "unqualified" for service in 2008, in part due to his admission of repeated marijuana use during the application process.

From February to September of 2010, while enrolled in Pima Community College, Loughner had several run-ins with college police for classroom and library disruptions. He was told that he needed to resolve his code of conduct violations and obtain a mental health clearance before being readmitted to the school.

According to a former friend, Loughner had a longstanding dislike for U.S. Representative Gabrielle Giffords, and had often expressed a view that women should not hold positions of power. He repeatedly derided Giffords as a "fake." He attended a rally she held in August, 2007, and was upset that she did not (in his view) adequately answer his question "What is government if words have no meaning?"[354]

On the morning of January 8, 2011 Loughner took a taxi to a Safeway supermarket location in Casas Adobes, where Rep. Giffords was holding a constituents meeting at the parking lot. About 20 to 30 people were gathered around a table set up outside the store.

At 10:10 am, Loughner opened fire on Giffords (the apparent target) as well as numerous bystanders, killing six people, one of whom was Chief U.S. District Judge John Roll.[355] Thirteen other people were injured by gunfire. Giffords was shot in the head and left in critical condition. Loughner proceeded to fire apparently randomly at other members of the crowd. Loughner was then subdued by bystanders and arrested by police.

Under the terms of a plea agreement, Loughner will most likely end his life in a prison psychiatric unit, with no possibility of parole.[356]

Run/Hide/FIGHT
Multiple individuals tackled gunman

A nearby store employee said he heard "15 to 20 gunshots." Loughner apparently stopped to reload, but dropped the magazine from his pocket to the sidewalk, and bystander Patricia Maisch grabbed it. Another bystander hit Loughner in the back of the head with a folding chair. The gunman was then tackled to the ground by 74-year-old retired U.S. Army Colonel Bill Badger (who himself had been shot), aided by Maisch and bystanders Roger Sulzgeber and Joseph Zamudio.[357]

Run/Hide/Fight/OTHER
Helped others

While waiting for help to arrive, Giffords' intern Daniel Hernandez, Jr. applied pressure to the gunshot wound to her head and made sure that she did not choke on her blood. Hernandez was credited with saving Giffords' life.[358]

Married doctor and nurse David and Nancy Bowman, who were shopping in the store, immediately set up triage and attended to nine-year-old Christina-Taylor Green, who died from her injury.[359]

Mass Shootings

Case #52 - IHOP Restaurant

Synopsis	Eduardo Sencion, 32, opened fire at an International House of Pancakes restaurant and later died from a self-inflicted gunshot.
Type of Establishment	Restaurant
Environment	Outdoors to indoors to outdoors
Motive	Unknown
Number killed	4
Number killed and injured	11
Date of murders	September 6, 2011
Weapon	Variant of AK-47 assault rifle
Location	Carson City, Nevada
Shooter status	Shot himself immediately afterward and died in hospital

Overview

Eduardo Sencion was born in Mexico and had a valid U.S. passport. He worked at a family business in South Lake Tahoe. He filed for bankruptcy protection in January 2009, listing more than $42,000 in outstanding debts for a car, several credit cards and some medical expenses. The case was discharged four months later.[360]

Just before 9:00 a.m. on September 6, 2011, Sencion pulled into the parking lot of an International House of Pancakes restaurant in Carson City, Nevada. Stepping out of his minivan, he opened fire at a man on a motorcycle, then entered the restaurant and went to a table of uniformed National Guard members, shooting each of them, three of whom were fatally wounded.[361]

Sencion then walked back to the parking lot and began firing into other businesses in the strip mall. He then shot himself in the head, and was later prounounced dead at a local hospital.[362]

Mass Shootings

Case #53 - SALON MERITAGE

Synopsis	Scott Evans Dekraai, 42, opened fire inside a hair salon and was later arrested.
Type of Establishment	Business
Environment	Indoors to outdoors
Motive	Domestic
Number killed	8
Number killed and injured	9
Date of murders	October 12, 2011
Weapons	9mm Springfield; Smith & Wesson .44 magnum; Heckler & Hoch .45
Location	Seal Beach, California
Shooter status	Indicted in January 2012 for eight counts of murder and one of attempted murder; as of this writing, in jail awaiting trial.[363]

Overview

Scott Evans Dekraai had lost a court case with his ex-wife Michelle involving their seven-year-old son. Michelle had claimed in court filings that her ex-husband was unstable and physically abusive to her during their marriage. Dekraai threatened violence.

At shortly after 1:00 p.m on October 12, 2011, he drove to the Salon Meritage, where his wife worked as a hairstylist, and opened fire on stylists and customers inside the shop, killing his ex-wife and six others. The shooting lasted approximately two minutes.[364]

Dekraai left the salon and headed to his vehicle. On the way, he encountered David Caouette, 64, who had been visiting the restaurant next door to the salon. Dekraai fired through the front windshield and passenger window of the vehicle, killing Caouette.[365]

Dekraai was arrested and surrendered without incident after being stopped about one half mile from the scene of the crime. He told police he had multiple weapons in his car.[366]

RUN/HIDE/Fight

Some of those inside the salon tried to escape by running into the street, locking themselves in private treatment rooms, or hiding in neighboring businesses.[367]

Run/HIDE/Fight

One employee who locked herself in one of the salon's rooms was unharmed. A man who locked himself in a bathroom was wounded.[368]

   Salon co-owner Sandy Fannin survived unharmed by hiding at the back of the property. Kimberly Criswell, owner of a nail salon two doors away said that when she and her customers heard gunshots. Her receptionist saw through the window as a man in the parking lot was shot. Criswell said, "We all ran into the bathroom and locked the door." [369]

Run/Hide/Fight/OTHER
Pled for life

Randy Fannin, the owner of Salon Meritage, was the first person to be shot, and died. He reportedly said to the gunman, "Please don't do this. There's another way. Let's go outside and talk." Dekraii said "Shut up" and continued firing.[370]

Case #54 - OIKOS UNIVERSITY

Synopsis	One L. Goh, 43, a former student, opened fire in a nursing classroom of a Korean Christian college. He fled the scene by car and was later arrested nearby.
Historical note	This was the deadliest outburst of gun violence at a U.S. school since the 2007 Virginia Tech massacre in which 32 people were killed.
Type of Establishment	University
Environment	Indoors
Motive	Revenge
Number killed	7
Number killed and injured	10
Date of murders	April 2, 2012
Weapon	45-caliber handgun
Location	Oakland, California
Shooter status	Arrested and charged with seven counts of murder and three counts of attempted murder. In January 2013 he was deemed unfit for trial due to diagnosis of paranoid schizophrenia. At the time of this writing, he was due to enter a treatment facility in an attempt to render him competent for trial.[371]

Overview

In 2009, One Goh had a failed marriage and a failed business. There were several court judgments and tax liens against him dating back to 2006. He owed more than $23,000 in federal taxes at one point and thousands of dollars more to banks and apartment owners. In an attempt to start over, he left Virginia and moved to California where his father lived.[372]

Goh enrolled in the nursing program at Oikos College, a Korean Christian college in Oakland. At 43, Goh was one of the most eager students in the nursing class. But he felt bullied and disrespected by his much-younger classmates, saying they made fun of his English-speaking skills.[373] Not long into the program, he dropped out and tangled with the administration in an effort to get back his $6,000 tuition.

On the morning of April 2, 2012, Goh arrived on campus with a .45 caliber handgun looking for a particular administrator. When he discovered that she was not in the building, he went into a classroom and told the students to stand up and line up against the wall. Then, when they would not all cooperate with his instructions, he opened fire.[374]

Goh fled the scene in a car belonging to one of the victims. He drove to a mall in Alameda, about five miles from the school, and told a security guard that he needed to speak to police because he had shot several people. He did not resist when taken into custody.[375]

RUN/Hide/Fight

Brian Snow was at a nearby credit union, when he first heard the shots and saw a victim run out of the building.[376]

Dawinder Kaar was shot in the arm as she stopped to help a friend who had fallen on the classroom/s floor; then she ran outside.[377]

Case #55 - Cafe Racer

Synopsis	Ian Stawicki, 40, gunned down four patrons at a café, and another person during a carjacking nearby, then shot himself as police closed in.
Type of Establishment	Restaurant
Environment	Indoors to outdoors
Motive	Retaliation
Number killed	5
Number killed and injured	7
Date of murders	May 30, 2012
Weapon	.45-caliber semi-automatic handgun
Location	Seattle, Washington
Shooter status	Committed suicide by shooting himself the same day

Overview

On May 30, 2012, Ian Stawicki's girlfriend thought he was acting "kind of crazy" and she would not let him have the car.[378] He apparently took his mother's car and went othe Café Racer in the University District of Seattle. Stawicki had been banned from the café for disruptive behavior, but came in anyway and attempted to place an order. After the barista declined to serve him, he opened fire with two .45 caliber handguns, killing four customers and wounding the café's chef.[379]

About a half-hour after the cafe shootings, Stawicki fatally shot Gloria Leonidas in a parking lot, then fled in her car. Later that afternoon, as police closed in on him, Stawicki knelt on a sidewalk in West Seattle and shot himself in the head.[380]

Run/**HIDE**/Fight

People scrambled for cover as soon as Stawicki began shooting.

One man calling 911 from Cafe Racer said, "Someone came in and shot a bunch of people. I'm hiding in the bathroom. We need help right away." [381]

Run/Hide/**FIGHT**

As the gunman aimed at him, one customer grabbed bar stools and threw them at Stawicki. The tactic created enough of a delay in the shooting that a few other customers were able to escape through the door which the gunman had blocked. [382]

"My brother died in the World Trade Center," the man later told police, who provided an account of the interview. After his brother's death, he said, he resolved that if something like this ever happened, I would never hide under a table" [383]

Run/Hide/**FIGHT**

Gloria Leonidas had just dropped off a friend in a parking lot when she was confronted by Stawicki. The gunman started beating her. Police said that she knocked the gun from his hand before he fatally shot her in the head. He then took off in her car. [384]

Run/Hide/Fight/**OTHER**
Bystanders helped

Even while Stawicki was still in the parking lot, a couple rushed across the street and began to administer CPR to Leonidas. [385]

Mass Shootings

Case #56 - CINEMARK MOVIE THEATER

Synopsis	James Holmes, 24, opened fire in a movie theater during the opening night of a movie, and was later arrested outside.
Historical note	The Cinemark rampage left the most victims of any mass shooting in U.S. history.
Type of Establishment	Movie theater
Environment	Indoors
Motive	Unknown
Number killed	12
Number killed and injured	70
Date of murders	July 20, 2012
Weapon	Smith & Wesson M&P15 rifle; Remington 870 Express tactical shotgun; 2 Glock .22 handguns
Location	Aurora, Colorado
Shooter status	In April 2013 Arapahoe County prosecutors announced that they would seek the death penalty for Holmes, with trial set for February 2014.[386]

Overview

James Holmes graduated from high school in San Diego, where his family still lived. He was a graduate student at the University of Colorado Denver/Anschutz Medical Campus but was in the process of withdrawing from the graduate program in neuroscience.[387]

Friday, July 20, 2012, marked a midnight screening of the latest Batman movie, *The Dark Knight Rises*, at the Cinemark movie theater in Aurora, Colorado. James Holmes bought a ticket and sat on the front row of the theater. About 20 minutes into the film, he left through an emergency exit door, which he propped open. He apparently then went to his car parked near the exit door, changed

Mass Shootings

into body armor and donned a gas mask, and reentered the theater through the door which he had propped open.[388]

Other audience members did not at first suspect anything dangerous, thinking it was just someone dressed in costume for the movie or part of a special event tied to the movie premiere.[389]

Holmes set off a canister of gas and opened fire with a variety of weapons. He fired a shotgun at the ceiling and then at the audiece. He also fired a semi-automatic rifle with 100-round drum magazine, which apparently malfunctioned after he began firing. Finally, Holmes fired a Glock 22 40-caliber handgun. He shot toward the back of the auditorium, then toward people in the aisles. One bullet passed through a wall and hit a person in the next theater.[390]

The first phone calls to emergency services were made at 12:39 a.m. Police arrived within 90 seconds. About 12:45 a.m., police apprehended Holmes behind the cinema, next to his car, without resistance.[391] His rampage had resulted in 12 dead and another 58 wounded.

RUN/Hide/Fight

Moviegoers fell to the floor and crawled over each other in an effort to get out. Some dragged bloodied bodies to the lobby.[392]

The man next to moviegoer Chris Ramos had already been shot, and others were falling. Ramos jammed his head down toward the floor and grabbed for his sister at the same time. "People were jumping over seats, jumping over you," Ramos said. On the floor, they felt bodies; as they crawled they came across a man with a bleeding leg wound. Ramos and his sister dragged the man as far as they could, and were eventually met in the lobby by police officers.[393]

Jennifer Seeger was sitting in the second row of the theater when the gunman burst in. He pointed a rifle at her face. She dove into the aisle and tucked herself under a chair, and Holmes shot a person behind her. "I had bullets that were on my forehead, burning my forehead, and I told myself, I need to get out of here...I crawled on the ground and I just laid in a ball and waited for him to go up the stairs," Seeger said, then told her friend that they had to leave. "At that point,

I was trying to crawl out but then everybody was crawling back in and saying, 'Don't go over there. He's going to shoot everybody trying to get out of the main doors,' and he was. All I hear is gunshot after gunshot. Just women and children are screaming."[394]

Patron Spenser Sherman recalled, "Everybody had dropped to the floor after the first couple gunshots, and then he fired some more. And then after that, there was a pause in the gunshots. But at that point, my boyfriend was like 'This is the time, we need to go, and we need to get out of the theater right now. So we ran."[395]

When the gunman tossed a smoke canister, Jordan Crofter ran for his life and was the first to make it to the lobby.[396]

Resharee Goodlo said, "I ran. I pushed. I did whatever I had to do to get out."[397]

Run/Hide/Fight/OTHER
Played dead

"I heard the gunshots...and I fell to the floor, crawling on the ground to try to get out," said moviegoer Corbin Dates said. As the gunman walked along the left side of the theater, Dates crawled up the right side, urging others to pretend that they were dead. He made it out, but saw bodies slumped over in their movie seats as he fled.[398]

Chandler Brannon, had been watching the movie with his girlfriend, and saw a smoke bomb go off and heard what sounded like fireworks. He then realized that the noises he was hearing were gunshots. "I told my girlfriend to just play dead," he said, adding that he never got a full view of the gunman. "All I could see was a silhouette."[399]

Mass Shootings

Case #57 - Sikh Temple

Synopsis	Wade Michael Page, 40, a white supremacist, opened fire in the parking lot of a Sikh temple, then went inside and shot congregants gathered prior to a service. He killed himself in the parking lot after being shot by a police officer.
Type of Establishment	Temple
Environment	Indoors
Motive	Domestic terrorism[400]
Number killed	6
Number killed and injured	9
Date of murders	August 5, 2012
Weapon	9mm semi-automatic handgun equipped with 19-round large capacity magazine
Location	Oak Creek, Wisconsin
Shooter status	Committed suicide after being shot by police at the scene.

Overview

Wade Michael Page was a U.S. Army veteran who others described as a "frustrated neo-Nazi." He had participated in several white supremacist rock bands with names like "Definite Hate," and had drawn the attention of groups that monitor extremist activity.[401]

On August 5, 2012, Page went to the Sikh temple in Oak Creek, Wisconsin and began shooting. He shot two people in the parking lot, then went inside the temple and continued to fire on people who were gathered to prepare for the Sunday service.

Page ambushed and opened fire on a veteran police officer who responded to the emergency and was attending to a victim on scene; the officer survived.[402]

Page killed himself in the parking lot after being shot by another police officer.[403]

Run/HIDE/Fight

Several children saw the gunman firing and alerted women who were cooking a meal for the service. Some hid in a pantry and were unharmed.[404]

Case #58 - Accent Signage Systems, Inc.

Synopsis	Andrew Engeldiner, 36, opened fire on employees at his workplace, then committed suicide.
Type of Establishment	Business
Environment	Indoors
Motive	Revenge
Number killed	5
Number killed and injured	9
Date of murders	September 27, 2012
Weapons	Glock 9mm handgun
Location	Minneapolis, Minnesota
Shooter status	Committed suicide by shooting himself the same day

Overview

Andrew Engeldinger was a longtime employee of Accent Signage Systems in Minneapolis who had clashed with superiors over poor performance and tardiness. He had struggled with paranoia and delusions, and had withdrawn from his family.

In September, 2012, Engeldinger had received a letter of reprimand which warned of possible termination. On September 27, he was asked to meet in John Souter's office. Engeldinger went to his car and returned with a Glock 9mm handgun. In the meeting, he was fired and was given his final paycheck. He pulled out the gun, and a struggle ensued between him, Souter, and employee Rami Cooks, and Souter and Cooks were wounded; Cook died.

Engeldinger reloaded and left Souter's office. Encountering company owner Reuven Rahamin, he shot him and went into the sales staff area. He shot and killed employee Jacob Beneke, then went to the loading dock area. There he shot employee Ron Edberg, as well as UPS driver Keith Basinki, who was in his truck at the dock area; both men died.

Engeldinger then went to the company's production area where he shot and wounded employee Eric River. Another employee was grazed by a bullet. Engeldinger then went to the basement and shot himself in the head.[405]

Run/Hide/**FIGHT**

Souter opened his office door to see Engeldinger raising a gun. Souter grabbed the barrel and pointed it upward as the gunman began firing. Souter was hit twice and fell.[406]

Case #59 - Sandy Hook Elementary School

Synopsis	Adam Peter Lanza, 20, fatally shot 20 children and 6 adults before killing himself at Sandy Hook Elementary School. Before driving to the school, he had shot and killed his mother.
Historical note	The Sandy Hook massacre was the second-deadliest school shooting in U.S. history, after the 2007 Virginia Teach massacre.
Type of Establishment	School
Environment	Indoors
Motive	Unknown
Number killed	27
Number killed and injured	29
Date of murders	December 14, 2012
Weapons	.22-caliber rifle; Bushmaster .223-caliber semi-automatic assault rifle equipped with 30-round large capacity ammunition magazine.[iv][407]
Location	Newtown, Connecticut
Shooter status	Committed suicide by shooting himself the same day

---

[iv] According to the Danbury State's Attorney, police also recovered in Lanza's possession a 9mm handgun and three loaded 30-round large-capacity ammunition magazines for the Bushmaster. Six additional 30-round large-capacity ammunition magazines were recovered at the scene. A loaded unknown make 12-gauge shotgun was found in Lanza's car. All of the guns used in the shooting were purchased by Lanza's mother.

Mass Shootings

Overview

Adam Peter Lanza lived with his mother in Newtown, Connecticut. He was a recluse who liked to play violent video games.[408] Sometime before 9:30 a.m. on December 14, 2012, Lanza shot his mother in the head multiple times at their home, then headed to Sandy Hook Elementary School which he had attended as a child.[409]

Wearing black military-style gear, including a bulletproof vest and mask, and using his mother's Bushmaster XM-15 rifle, Lanza shot his way through a locked glass door at the front of the school and started shooting, continuing for 15 to 20 minutes and firing between 50 and 100 rounds. He shot all of his victims multiple times, mostly in two first-grade classrooms, killing 14 children in one room and six in the other. The student victims were eight boys and twelve girls, between six and seven years of age, and the six adults were all women who worked at the school. Lanza shot himself in the head as first responders arrived.[410]

Investigators later found weapons at the Lanza home incuding a 7-foot pole with a blade on one side and a spear on another; a metal bayonet; three samurai swords; a .323-caliber bolt-action rifle; a .22 caliber Savage Mark II rifle; and a .22 caliber Volcanic starter pistol. Literature removed from the house included a news article on the 2008 shooting at Northern Illinois University and a National Rifle Association guide to pistol shooting.[411]

Run/HIDE/Fight

A teacher and students took refuge in a gymnasium closet.[412]

School nurse Sarah Cox hid under a desk in her office, and saw Lanza enter her office and stand 20 feet away before turning around and leaving. Cox and school secretary Barbara Halstead then hid in a first-aid supply closet for up to four hours, after calling 9-1-1.[413]

First grade teacher Kaitlin Roig hid 14 students in a bathroom and barricaded the door, telling them to be completely quiet to remain safe.[414]

School library staff Yvonne Cech and Maryann Jacob tried to hide 18 children in an area of the library which was used for lockdown in practice drills, but on discovering that one of the doors would not lock, they had the children crawl into a storage room. Cech barricaded the door with a filing cabinet.[415]

Music teacher Maryrose Kristopik barricaded her fourth-grader students in a small supply closet. Lanza arrived moments later, pounding and yelling "Let me in", while the students in Kristopik's class quietly hid inside.[416]

Two third graders, chosen as classroom helpers, were walking down the hallway to the office to deliver the morning attendance sheet during the shooting. Teacher Abbey Clements pulled both children into her classroom, where they hid. They were unharmed.[417]

Reading specialist Laura Feinstein grabbed two students from outside her classroom and hid with them under desks after they heard gunshots. Feinstein called the school office and attempted to call 9-1-1 but was unable to connect because her cell phone did not have reception. She hid with the children for approximately 40 minutes, before law enforcement came to lead them out of the room.[418]

Teacher Victoria Soto attempted to hide several children in a closet and cupboards. As Lanza entered her classroom, Soto reportedly told him that the children were in the auditorium. Several of the children then came out of their hiding place and tried to run for safety and were shot dead. Soto got between the students and Lanza, who then fatally shot her. {After the shooting, six surviving children from Soto's class crawled out of the cupboards and fled the school. As reported by his parents, a 6-year-old boy in Ms. Soto's class fled with a group of his classmates and the children escaped through the door when the gunman shot their teacher.}[419]

Run/Hide/Fight/OTHER
Confronted gunman

School principal Dawn Hochsprung, and school psychologist Mary Sherlach were meeting with other faculty members when they heard gunshots outside. Hochsprung and Sherlach left the room and rushed toward the sounds and encountered Lanza, who shot both women dead as they confronted him.[420]

Run/Hide/Fight/OTHER
Alerted others

A custodian ran through hallways, alerting classrooms.[421]

Run/Hide/Fight/OTHER
Tried to protect others

Teacher Natalie Hammond was in a faculty meeting when gunshots were heard. She pressed her body against the door to keep it closed. Lanza shot through the door, hitting Hammond in the leg and arm.[422]

Teacher's aide Anne Marie Murphy shielded a 6-year-old boy with her body; the bullets killed them both.[423]

Paraprofessional Rachel D'Avino had been employed at the school for just over a week, also died trying to protect her students.[424]

Run/Hide/Fight/OTHER
Played dead

First-grade substitute teacher Lauren Rousseau was shot in the face and killed. All but one of the children in her classroom were also shot dead. The sole survivor, a six-year-old girl, played dead and remained still until the building was quiet and she thought it was safe to leave. Covered in blood, she was the first child to escape the building.[425]

Unique observations of actions taken by survivors of mass shootings

After reviewing each of the case studies and analyzing them through the prism of three decades in law enforcement, several commonalities became evident with regard to the instinctive actions taken and conscious tactics implemented by victims of mass shooting attacks. Some instinctual actions were the correct path to safety, while others may have increased the level of victimization.

This section examines some of the common victim responses—whether instinctive or conscious—and how those actions or tactics helped or hurt those involved.

For example: for years, academicians have told us that one of our most basic instincts when faced with imminent danger is "fight or flight." These instinctual actions are also two-thirds of the DHS Active Shooter Response Model. However, research clearly indicates that fighting—especially by an untrained, unarmed individual—rarely results in a safe and successful conclusion to the event. Actually, this type of response almost always leads to the injury or death of the individual attempting to stop the shooter's rampage. More detailed information on fighting an armed offender as a response during a mass shooting is presented in the ENGAGE portion of the ESCAPE Model later in this text.

On the other hand, certain tactics such as playing dead have worked on multiple occasions by a wide range of individuals, some of whom stated that they saw the tactic on television, and others who just thought it seemed like a good idea at the time. Other tactics which seem just as reasonable, such as pleading for one's life, have failed the majority of the time.

Armed with these vital observations, citizens will be able to learn from past incidents, and understand both successful and unsuccessful tactics which have been utilized by victims in such events.

Mass Shootings

Successful Tactics

An examination of successful tactics taken by individuals who have survived a mass shooting reveals that:

- Locked or barricaded doors can slow or stop offenders; and
- Playing dead (whether actually wounded or not) can save your life.

Both of these tactics have been successfully employed by victims during mass shootings or active shooter incidents.

1. *Locked/barricaded doors can slow or stop offenders*

On multiple occasions, especially in schools and workplaces, locking or barricading doors has proven to be a highly successful tactic. If you have an opportunity to lock the door with the offender on the outside, **do so immediately.** If you do not feel that the lock will stop the shooter and you can safely move to barricade the door with chairs, tables, couches or other furniture, then do so.

You may be able to topple file cabinets (even if heavy) or other large items in order to impede the shooter's path towards you. Often these obstructions will also serve as either cover or concealment and may frustrate the shooter in his attempt to enter so that he moves on to easier targets.

Remember, mass shootings are usually not prolonged events. They often take less than 12 minutes, so the offender usually does not have (or take) the time to shoot open a door and knock down a barricade in order to make entry. Reports from survivors often recount how the shooter tried the lock or pushed on the door, but when unable to gain entry simply moved on, sparing the occupants inside. This is one of the main reasons school districts throughout the

Mass Shootings

country practice lockdown procedures, and why corporations should implement these same successful tactics.[v]

Case #37. An attempt to break into an English classroom was thwarted by a quick-thinking teacher who had taken the precaution to lock the door. This execution of one of the safety procedures established by the school saved many lives.

Case #53. The owner of a salon two doors away from the location of the shootings said she and her customers and employees heard gunshots, and her receptionist saw a man through a window as he was shot in a parking lot. "There was like a pop, pop and my receptionist screamed,'he just shot that man' and we all ran into the bathroom and locked the door," Kimberly Criswell said.

Case #59. First grade teacher Kaitlin Roig hid 14 students in a bathroom and barricaded the door, telling them to be completely quiet to remain safe.

2. *Playing dead has worked on a number of occasions*

From the case analyses, I was surprised to discover that playing dead provided an extremely high survival chance during a shooting incident, whether the victims were previously injured or not. Upon closer analysis of these events I realized that there is more than reasonable logic behind such a finding: during a mass shooting incident, especially when the shooter has a large number of targets (people) from which to choose, playing dead would draw the least attention from the shooter.

Often shooters appear to be on a "mission" to kill as many people as possible. If they believe they have already fatally wounded their targets, they may simply keep moving on to other victims instead of ensuring that those already shot are dead.

---

[v] NOTE: Many of the case references which follow appeared in the previous Case Studies and are referenced in the End Notes. Those anecdotes or reports which did not appear in previous chapters will show End Note references here.

Mass Shootings

Similar in nature to a locked door which slows down the attacker, most shooters move quickly through a location and do not take the time to check on each and every victim. The possible exception to this might be if the shooter had a specific target or primary victim(s) in mind, such a student who bullied them or a boss who fired them, and they wanted to ensure that their attack had been successfully concluded.

It is important to note that there appears to be no unified explanation as to why certain people decided to play dead. Some did it as a result of extreme fear, some did it because of they were badly injured or immobilized, and some did it as a conscious strategy to stay alive.

Case #4. Joshua Coleman, 11, was riding his bike to McDonald's and heard the [shooter] yell. He turned and he was hit. Lying on the pavement, his right side riddled with shotgun pellets, and the gunman still shooting, Joshua played dead. How did he know to do so? "I don't know," he says. "I got lucky. The fact he kept shooting at us... You hear about an accident and sometimes you think, 'What would you do if you were there?' and I always thought I would play dead."

Case #16. The first gunshot victim, Mary Anne Phillips, testified that she had played dead after being wounded. She said she kept her eyes closed so that [the shooter] would not come back and shoot her again.

Case #21. Lelan Brookins survived the massacre by playing dead.

Case #27. Isaiah Shoels, Matthew Kechter and Craig Scott were hiding underneath a table. Harris knelt down and shot Shoels once in the chest at close range, killing him. Klebold also knelt down and opened fire, hitting and killing Matthew Kechter. Craig Scott lay next to his friends and played dead and was uninjured.

Mark Taylor was shot in the chest, arms and leg and fell to the ground, where he played dead and survived.

Case #37. Lance Crowe, 15, survived by playing dead, lying among those killed.

Case #48. Receptionist Shirley DeLucia was one of the first to be shot, being hit in the stomach. She then pretended to be dead and, when the gunman moved on, hid under a desk and called 911.

Case #56. Moviegoer Corbin Dates crawled on the floor to try to get out. He urged others to pretend that they were dead.

Chandler Brannon realized that the noises he was hearing were gunshots. "I told my girlfriend to just play dead," he said.

Case #59. First grade substitute teacher Lauren Rousseau and all but one of the children in her classroom were shot dead. The sole survivor, a six-year-old girl, played dead and remained still until the building was quiet and she thought it was safe to leave. She was the first child to escape the building.

Most Common Concerns

An examination of actions taken by those involved in mass shootings revealed two primary areas of concern:

1. Pleading for your life rarely works, and

2. Not realizing what was occurring slowed the responses by individuals.

Becoming aware of these facts will add to your personal database of knowledge and, ideally, better prepare you if you are ever faced with a mass shooting incident.

Pleading for your life rarely works

There have been numerous cases where individuals caught in the killer's line of sight with nowhere to run or hide have pled for their lives or the lives of others. More often than not, those pleas fell on deaf ears—or, more correctly, on non-empathetic ears.

Mass Shootings

For years researchers studying the psychology of various types of killers have listed a <u>lack of empathy for others</u> as a common characteristic. Because of this lack of compassion for others, it should not come as a surprise that pleading for one's life is often a futile tactic. Most of these killers act as if they are on a mission with a goal of securing as high a body count as possible. Seldom over the past 30 years has a mass murderer decided to spare someone's life in an out-of- character act of compassion.

Additionally, individuals who unnecessarily exposed themselves to the assailant to beg for mercy for themselves or others often found themselves targeted, with the ultimate result that they became a victim. If one understands an offender's lack of empathy for his victims, then <u>any</u> other decision, such as remaining concealed or playing dead, may provide a better opportunity for survival.

Case #15. Restaurant proprietor Pete Parrous approached [the gunman] and asked him not to hurt anyone. Parrous was shot in the face and died instantly. As he fell, his wife stood up screaming and she was shot too. She fell beside her daughter, who began screaming and who was shot in the thigh.

Wesley Cover had been tending to a patron who had been hit by a pellet from the shooting. He asked the gunman not to hurt the woman he was helping because she was pregnant. Mr. Cover was then shot in the head and died. The woman was also shot, but not fatally.

Case #17. Customer Colleen O'Connor saw [the gunman] coming and knelt in front of him to beg for her life. As she raised her arms, he held a gun just 18 inches from her head. "Don't shoot," she cried. "I won't tell." "I have to," the shooter said as he pulled the trigger.

Case #24. Lottery president Otho Brown ran from the building with Beck in pursuit. Brown stumbled in the parking lot, apparently after losing a shoe. He fell to the ground, raised his hands, and begged "Don't kill me, don't kill me," to which Beck answered, "Aw, shut up," and shot him.

Case #53. Randy Fannin...was the first person to be shot, and died. He reportedly said to the gunman, "Please don't do this. There's another way. Let's go outside and talk." Dekraii [the gunman] said "Shut up" and continued firing.

Not realizing what was occurring slowed responses by individuals

In conducting research for this book, reading through each of the cases in rapid succession without trying to consciously look for commonalities or attempting to over-process the information, I found that several themes became quite evident. One of the most common occurrences was that at the beginning of a shooting, it took some people a moment to realize a shooting had occurred. I contend that the reason for the delayed response is that most people have never heard gunfire or been involved in any type of violent incident.

On numerous occasions, victims mistook gunfire or even explosions as firecrackers, pranks or part of some type of play, holiday celebration or promotional stunt, causing their initial response to be delayed by valuable seconds or even minutes.

In a mass shooting situation, every second counts and even the slightest delay in response can have dire consequences. It is for this reason that after the Columbine massacre law enforcement agencies throughout the county changed their policies and procedures in an effort to speed up response to active shooter events. Response time is critical during these situations, and new active shooter protocols are centered on dynamic entry to reduce response time and quickly conclude the incident.

Individuals must be able to quickly recognize the situation and respond. If you are a teacher in a school, an employee in a post office, or a worker in an office building and hear sounds similar to gunshots, you should recognize that firecrackers or other pyrotechnics are not normal for your workplace, and immediately take action by implementing the ESCAPE Model presented in this book.

Mass Shootings

Case #8. One schoolchild stated that students panicked. "Everybody just got down because they didn't know what was happening; everyone started screaming."

Case #16. Initially, some passengers mistook the gunshots for caps or fireworks, until a woman shouted, "He's got a gun! He's shooting people!" Other passengers farther away in the train did not realize a shooting had occurred until after the train stopped.[426]

Case #25. "We thought it was just firecrackers," said one student.

Case #26. Several students said they thought the shooting was a gag related to student-body election day. "I thought it was fake. I had never heard a gun go off," Stephani Quimby said. "It was like a movie and you were there...I knew it was real when I saw him point the gun at someone and hear a girl yell, 'Tressa!' I knew she wouldn't joke."[427]

Case #29. Some 150 teenagers gathered inside initially thought the killer was part of a skit as he began cursing and spouting anti-Baptist rhetoric.

Case #31. Waitress Kathy Pruniski heard sounds and assumed they were part of the holiday celebrations at the hotel. "Isn't that funny, they're getting a jump on New Year's," she said to some guests. "I thought they were playing some game," {one} said.

Diana Izquierdo was just about to leave with her mother when the shots started. "I thought it was firecrackers," she said.[428]

Case #33. Bryan Snyder, shot in the left arm, said that he thought at first the attack was a prank. "It was completely unreal," Snyder said. When co-worker Carl Swanson fell to the floor, Snyder said he thought his colleague was playing around. Then two shots whizzed by Snyder, and a third tore through his upper arm. Even as he rolled to the floor, Snyder said he was convinced the man, whom he had never seen before, had shot him with a paintball gun.[429]

Case #37. Wounded student Cody Thunder said, "At first, I thought he was messing around. I thought it was a paintball gun or something."[430]

Case #44. Shawn Vidlak said the shots sounded like a nail gun, and thought it was noise from construction work. "People started screaming about gunshots," Vidlak said. "I grabbed my wife and kids. We got out of there as fast as we could."

"All of us were slightly confused because we didn't know what it was," said one mall employee about the first burst of gunfire.[431]

Case #46. "It was just surreal," according to junior Dan Sweeney. "Even when the first shot was fired I couldn't believe it was happening. It didn't seem to register with anyone."

"It didn't even sound like I thought a gun would sound like," said senior Desiree Smith. "It sounded like a cork coming out of a champagne bottle." [432]

Harold Ng said the danger didn't even register even after the firing started. "I was still in the dream state and I didn't think it was reality. It was like a video game," he said.

Case #53. A woman...was having her hair done when the gunman opened fire. "We thought it was maybe firecrackers," she said.[433]

Case #56. When Holmes re-entered the theater through the exit door, initially, few in the audience considered the masked figure a threat. He appeared to be wearing a costume, like other audience members who had dressed up for the screening. Some believed that the gunman was playing a prank, while others thought that he was part of a special effects installation set up for the film's premiere as a publicity stunt by the studio or theater management.

When Chris Ramos first saw the gunman come through the exit door, he saw objects flying in the air and thought they were fake bats, all in the spirit of the hour.[434]

Corbin Dates said that when he saw the theater's emergency doors swing open and a man walk inside, he thought it was some kind of movie-related stunt. Even as people screamed, he thought it was part of the show.[435]

Salina Jordan was in the next theater…when she heard a series of pops. "It was so in synch we thought it was part of the movie," said Jordan. "We thought it was a special effect because they were trying to do it up big for opening night." [436]

ESCAPE: A Six Step Model for Survival

Although in the past few years there have been many articles, news accounts and blogs written about mass shootings in the United States, most of these stories have focused on the actions taken by the assailants, the types of weapons used, or the individual circumstances of the event.

After nearly 30 years in law enforcement, serving in positions from Police Officer to Chief of Police, and having trained thousands of officers as a certified police instructor, I was interested in learning if there were specific and identifiable commonalities in the actions taken and tactics employed by those individuals who had firsthand experience as victims of mass shootings. If so, would I be able to isolate those commonalities and develop a model based on successful actions and tactics that could be used to teach others?

During the 1990's I conducted similar research into the actions taken by teachers and administrators at various school shootings which had occurred during that decade. As a result I developed the easy-to-remember four-step RAIN Model (*Respond, Assess, Isolate* and *Notify*). This model provided educators who had a "duty to protect" with precise actions to take during a school shooting or other violent incident in order to mitigate the harm and save lives. This model has subsequently been taught to thousands of school personnel in hundreds of districts throughout the country, and is still featured in the book *School Safety 101: Preparing Schools and Protecting Students* (3rd Edition).

When I began research for this book on mass shootings, I wondered if such a model was possible given the ever-changing dynamics of a mass shooting situation and the wide diversity of people and places involved. In school shootings, the locations were static in nature and the victim pool similar. Would such a model be possible when offenders ranged from mere children to senior citizens, and locations varied from shopping malls to business offices, from schools to civic buildings?

Mass Shootings

Obviously the answer was yes, but I was amazed to discover it was a resounding YES. The actions taken and the decisions made by those who survived these violent incidents provided me with more than enough information to use to develop a replicable and teachable model, a model that can be taught in an age-appropriate manner to nearly everyone in any environment. I hope that throughout the country in workplaces, schools, churches, shopping malls or festivals, wherever people gather, they can apply this model and these lessons learned in order to give themselves and their loved ones a better chance at surviving a mass shooting.

> **NOTE:** An active shooter situation is dynamic and ever-changing. Actions taken by victims must be based on the information they have at the time of the event, making the best decisions possible based on the circumstances and the totality of the information available.

The following six step model is based on research of the actions taken by victims of previous mass shooting attacks:

Exit when possible without presenting a target;

Seek cover to protect yourself from harm;

Conceal yourself from the offenders;

Assess all alternatives;

Present a small target;

Engage, only as a last resort.

EXIT
S
C
A
P
E

- AS SOON AS POSSIBLE WHEN SAFE TO DO SO
- WITHOUT PRESENTING A TARGET FOR THE SHOOTER
- WITHOUT DRAWING ATTENTION TO YOURSELF

As the previous case illustrations made clear, on many occasions victims mistook gunfire as firecrackers, or actions by the gunman as a skit or part of a staged presentation. One assumption is that few people are actually familiar with the sounds of live gunfire, and therefore they assume the best and not the worst. Couple this with the fact that most people never believe that they will be in an active shooter situation, or that an event such as a mass shooting could ever happen in their community, and it is easy to see that the average citizen can't believe what they are seeing and hearing.

When confronted with a mass shooting you must take immediate action. You cannot "freeze up" or "freak out," as survivors have described their responses. You must try to remain calm, keep your wits about you, and immediately take action by exiting the location as soon as possible. **Exiting the location and removing yourself from the violent incident is the single most important action for surviving a mass shooting event.**

But exiting is not as simple as just jumping up from your chair and running away from the scene. You must make intelligent choices concerning escape. The autonomic response of "flight" sounds simple, but to survive an attack by an active shooter is significantly more complex.

Mass Shootings

Simply getting up and fleeing could be the worst action to take if you then present a target to the offender or draw his attention toward you. Based on the specific circumstances presented, you may have to crawl on your knees or belly, or hide until the shooter's attention is diverted away from you, and then crawl or run to safety. In open spaces you may have to zigzag or vary your running pattern; when indoors, moving in short bursts from one position of cover or concealment to another may be your best option.

If you are sitting or standing by an exit and the gunman is not immediately in front of you or staring at you, exit as quickly as possible and run as far from the scene as possible. DO NOT wait and see what the gunman is going to do next or what is going to happen to others. Leave the scene immediately and do not attempt to move wounded individuals.

If you have small children try to pick them up and run with them; otherwise drop everything else—purses, handbags, computers—in order to be as mobile as possible. While exiting, keep your hands in plain sight or over your head if ordered to do so by responding officers.

If practical, shed high heels or long coats which may impede your ability to quickly escape from the scene. Remember, *your life is at stake* and any item that slows you down makes you more susceptible to becoming a victim.

Once you have cleared the scene, call 911 to ensure that assistance is coming. *Never assume that someone else has called 911.*

What to Report when Calling 911:

- Your specific location, with building name and office or classroom number if applicable.
- Number of people at your specific location
- Injuries, with number of people injured and types of injuries

Note: If possible and when safe to do so, the dispatcher may provide instructions on how to care for injured until medical assistance can be provided.

- The shooter(s):
  - Specific location
  - Number of shooter(s)
  - Race and gender
  - Physical features–height, weight, facial hair, glasses
  - Clothing color and style
  - Backpack or other type of bag?
  - Type of weapons (rifle/shotgun, handgun) if known
  - Do you recognize the shooter? What's his/her name?
  - Have you heard explosions separate from gunshots?

If you can't speak, leave the line open so the dispatcher can listen to what is taking place. This is an effective technique which has been utilized in schools to alert both students and teachers, and one that has been used for years by police officers who find themselves in dangerous situations and need to alert other officers of their need for assistance.

Remember: *the single best response to an active shooter situation is to exit the location as quickly and safely as possible.* Let's look at some examples.

- **AS SOON AS POSSIBLE WHEN SAFE TO DO SO**

Case #56. Spenser Sherman recalled, "Everybody had dropped to the floor after the first couple gunshots, and then he fired some more. And then after that, there was a pause in the gunshots. But at that point, my boyfriend was like 'This is the time, we need to go, and we need to get out of the theater right now. So we ran."

- **WITHOUT PRESENTING A TARGET FOR THE SHOOTER**

Case #46. Desiree Smith said, "I dropped to the ground under my seat, and could see another girl down there. We just stared at each other... Then we moved all of a sudden. Everyone was army-crawling toward the back of the auditorium on the floor. As soon as I reached the door, I got halfway hunched over, and then started to run as soon as I got outside."

- **WITHOUT DRAWING ATTENTION TO YOURSELF**

Case #4. 11-year-old Aurora lay on the restaurant floor, her eyes closed tight, afraid to look. "I thought I heard him far away, so I opened my eyes and he saw me. He walked to the trash can and he had some {guns} in there. He got his shotgun. That's when he shot me."

Case #5. The gunman chased a group of fleeing employees out a side exit, shooting one man, who later died in the parking lot.

Case #56. Moviegoers dropped to the floor and crawled over one another in an effort to get out.

E
SEEK COVER FOR PROTECTION
C

A

P

E

Although one's initial goal may be to seek concealment or hide from the offender, an even safer course of action is to **seek cover**.

The difference between cover and concealment is that while *concealment* simply hides you, *cover* will provide you protection from bullets. Common examples of cover found in public places include: parked cars, cement barriers in parking lots, brick walls, concrete support poles, or structural steel beams.

If these types of structures are not available, look for low places in the ground which might provide protection. This could be natural indentations in the ground, in drainage ditches, sewer culverts, or even laying prone on the ground alongside a cement curb in a parking lot.

Concealment such as bushes, signs or banners or even smoke will visually screen you from the offender's line of sight but will not provide protection from bullets. *Cover* will stop bullets or increase the level of protection for victims seeking refuge behind these objects.

In an office or workplace, most desks do not provide cover. However, items such as file cabinets, large pieces of machinery made of steel, or other metal objects may provide protection from the attack. Structurally, most interior walls will provide a minimum of cover while exterior walls—especially those with either a brick or cinder block construction—will provide a maximum of protection from bullets of nearly any caliber. Structural support beams of either wood or steel will provide cover, as will various types of fencing and even landscape features such as retaining walls and thick trees.

Mass Shootings

Obviously, the best situation possible for a person involved in a mass shooting event who cannot safely exit the area would be to conceal himself in a place that also provides the proper amount of cover from the offender's weapons of death.

Case #5. {An} employee escaped by locking herself in a vault where stamps are kept. Two other survivors hid in a broom closet.

Case #29. Some 150 teenagers gathered inside initially thought the killer was part of a skit…. They scrambled for cover as Ashbrook opened fire.

A boulder can provide cover

Trees can provide cover

A culvert can provide cover

A brick wall or column can provide cover

E
S
CONCEAL YOURSELF
A
P
E

- **CONCEAL YOURSELF - HIDE FROM THE OFFENDER(S)**
- **HIDING IN AN OPEN AREA UNDER TABLES AND CHAIRS IS NOT GOOD ENOUGH**
- **BE CREATIVE IN FINDING PLACES TO HIDE**
- **REMAIN HIDDEN UNTIL RESCUED BY POLICE**

If during a mass shooting or active shooter attack it is impossible to safely exit from the location or to find protective cover, the next best option is to conceal yourself from the offender. As has been noted, mass shootings are dynamic events where the shooter is actively pursuing easy targets. Since the offender often moves quickly from target to target, it is hoped that he will pass by concealed individuals, not bothering to take the time to seek them out.

If faced with a mass shooting situation, find a place to hide and then **stay hidden** until it is safe to move. Find a closet, bathroom, cabinet or storage room: whatever is available at the time, accessible at the moment, and maybe most important: out of the offender's line of sight.

In several cases individuals who ducked under a desk or table but who were still within the shooter's line of sight were systematically gunned down as the offender moved through the area.

If you find yourself in a school or office cafeteria or a food court at the mall, and your only option is to dive under the table, try to keep moving by rolling on the ground or "army-crawling" in an effort to hide from the shooter.

If you are outside and need to find concealment, consider hiding behind a row of bushes, under a pile of trash or debris, or even in a drainage ditch; these all are viable options in a life and death situation. Sometimes you may need to hide from the offender just long enough for him to lose track of you as he moves on to another target.

Under certain conditions, even areas with shadows can provide you some concealment from the shooter. This is especially true in outdoor situations where the shooter is in the bright sunlight and moving quickly between locations. Moving into the shadows may provide just enough concealment to allow you to escape harm.

Even shadows can conceal you

Mass Shootings

During such a life-and-death encounter, you may be uncomfortable for a few minutes or even longer, but you must try to remain calm and quiet until you can safely move to more protective cover or exit the situation entirely. If you are a caretaker for another person such as a young child or elderly adult, try to encourage them to be as still and as silent as possible so as not to draw the attention of the shooter.

Ground cover can provide concealment

During a shooting you may only have seconds to hide. If it is possible, be creative and secrete yourself in a location where the offender will not take the time to look for you. Some ingenious places survivors have found to hide include a vault, a freezer, and even a commercial dishwasher. In each of these cases the individual survived the attack unharmed.

Once hidden, stay there until an opportunity to safely exit the scene presents itself, you can safely make it to a position that also provides cover, or you are rescued by first responders. DO NOT be impatient and try to run just because you no longer see the shooter or hear gunshots. In many cases the offender left the building and then returned to continue his assault; or simply paused to re-load his weapon, causing a lull in the action but not ending the attack.

Case #42. **Kevin Granata and Wally Grant left the locked room and went downstairs to investigate. Both were shot.**

In some instances survivors remained concealed for hours until they were sure the police were on the scene and the attack had ceased. Prematurely leaving a well-concealed place may expose one to the offender and have deadly consequences.

If your school or workplace has a lockdown procedure, it should be implemented as soon as possible in the event of an attack. A lockdown procedure may be implemented when a situation occurs that may be an imminent hazard to health, or is life threatening. It is intended to limit access and hazards by controlling and managing staff, students or other building occupants in order to increase safety and reduce possible victimization. The entire facility should have restricted access until the "All Clear" is given, or individuals are directed by emergency personnel or staff based on pre-established procedures.

Actions to minimize attention from the shooter during a lockdown:

- Proceed to a room that can be locked, close and lock all windows and doors, turn off all lights. Also block the door using whatever is available (i.e. furniture).
- Close blinds.
- Turn off radios and computer monitors if necessary.
- Silence cell phones.
- Keep occupants calm and quiet.
- Position people out of sight and behind items that might offer additional protection (walls, desks, file cabinets, etc.).
- If there is nothing to hide behind, get everyone down on the floor and ensure that no one is visible from outside the room.
- When safe, call 911, advise the police of the incident and your location, remain in place until police or a familiar person arrives, and gives the all clear using pre-established protocols.

When utilizing formal lockdown procedures, never leave your safe and secure position until rescued, or proper release procedures are followed. If you do not have lockdown protocols established, you should remain in a safe area until rescued by police. You must be cognizant of the fact that the shooter will not stop until his objectives have been met, unless he is engaged by law enforcement.

Before leaving your safe position, consider the risk of exposure created by opening the door. Remember that attempts to rescue people should only be made if that can be done without further endangering the persons inside a secured area.

- **CONCEAL YOURSELF, HIDE FROM THE OFFENDER**

Case #27. Teacher Patti Nielson dialed 911 and concealed herself underneath the library's administrative counter. Brian Anderson escaped to the library where he concealed himself inside an open staff break room.

Case #48. Some of those present managed to escape to a basement, while more than a dozen hid in a closet.

Case #53. One of the employees involved locked herself in the salon's facial room and was unharmed. Another man locked himself in a bathroom but was wounded.

Two doors away, the owner of a salon and her employees ran into the bathroom and locked the door.

Case #55. One man calling 911 from Café Racer said, "Someone came in and shot a bunch of people. I'm hiding in the bathroom."

Case #59. A teacher and students took refuge in a gymnasium closet.

School nurse Sarah Cox hid under a desk in her office...She and school secretary Barbara Halstead then hid in a first-aid supply closet for up to four hours, after calling 911.

Mass Shootings

First grade teacher Kaitlin Roig hid 14 students in a bathroom and barricaded the door, telling them to be completely quiet to remain safe.

Library staff Yvonne Cech and Maryann Jacob first hid 18 children in a part of the library the school used for lockdown in practice drills...[then] had the children crawl into a storage room. Cech barricaded the door with a filing cabinet.

Teacher Maryrose Kristopik barricaded her fourth-graders in a tiny supply closet. Lanza arrived moments later, pounding and yelling "Let me in," while the students...quietly hid inside.

- **HIDING UNDER TABLES AND CHAIRS IN OPEN AREAS IS NOT GOOD ENOUGH**

On several occasions, both in school cafeterias and in office buildings where individuals hid under desks, behind chairs or underneath tables—but in places which were still in the shooter's line of sight—the offender shot through or under the furniture, effectively "executing" those within.

Case #3. Witness Terry Rippa said he was just reaching for money to pay his bar bill when he heard the gunshots. "We went under the table, and the guy went one, two, three, four, five down the row," Rippa said.

Case #5. {The gunman} bolted several doors and then systematically searched the workroom floor for workers who were cowering under tables and in cubicles. He killed three people in one work station and five in another.

Case #10. When someone hollered "Get down!" some realized what was happening and dived under desks to escape. There they were trapped. Pough {the gunman} started picking off those ducking for cover.

• BE CREATIVE IN FINDING PLACES TO HIDE

The best way to be creative in finding places to hide is **before an attack occurs**. In both law enforcement and military circles this tactic is referred to as "situational awareness." This involves knowing one's surroundings and making deliberate decisions beforehand on possible routes of escape, places for cover and concealment, and in some cases even sizing up possible offenders as a threat.

For the average person, situational awareness can be as simple as surveying your surroundings in an unfamiliar place for exit routes and making a mental note of places that might provide cover or concealment. One example of situational awareness which occurs hundreds of times a day for airline passengers is when the flight attendant calls travelers' attention to the escape doors, the lighted paths that lead to the exits, and the oxygen masks that will deploy under certain conditions. Whether in a restaurant, shopping mall or school, everyone should be able to practice some level of situational awareness.

Case #4. When the shooting started, {one} employee and a co-worker fled to a basement utility room, where they were joined by three female co-workers, a woman with a baby, and a man who was bleeding. They huddled in the hot basement with gunfire sounding overhead. Finally, police knocked at the door, and though they were fearful, they opened it.

Case #5. "I heard a gunshot, and hid behind some big boxes. I looked up and saw a man shooting a gun. He...then just turned in a circle shooting at random. He went towards the front lobby shooting and we ran out the back."

"I hid under my case and behind the parcel tub."

"I ran around behind some rural carrier cases trying to hide."

Two other survivors hid in a broom closet.

Tracy Sanchez and another man tried to flee through the back door, but it was locked. "We ran back and there was a storage closet nearby. We hid in there, but we couldn't lock it so we turned the light off and stayed quiet...we stayed hidden until we heard the police." [437]

Case #6. Three people huddled together unhurt in a refrigerated storeroom.

Case #11. One woman survived by hiding in a freezer. A food preparer escaped by hiding inside an industrial dishwasher.

Case #44. Shopper Jennier Kramer said, "We hid in a pants rack towards the back of the men's department."

Case #53. One employee who locked herself in one of the salon's rooms was unharmed. A man who locked himself in a bathroom was wounded. The salon owner survived unharmed by hiding at the back of the property.

- **REMAIN HIDDEN UNTIL RESCUED BY POLICE**

The last aspect of concealing oneself is to <u>remain hidden</u> until rescued by police or other first responders. If you are in a safe and secure position, wait patiently—do not move until ordered to do so. Do not respond to any voice commands until you can verify them with certainty, because an unfamiliar voice may be the shooter attempting to lure victims from their safe space. This includes responding to announcements made over intercom or public address systems.

Schools and workplaces should have crisis response plans for concluding a lockdown without utilizing mass communications systems, since such systems can be compromised by offenders gaining access to the communications or forcing others to make false safety announcements.

Case #4. Employee Ken Dickey and {others} fled to a basement utility room. They remained in the basement until police knocked at the door.

Case #27. Teacher Patti Nielson and several others locked themselves in a break room, and stayed there until they were freed, hours after the attack began.

Case #41. For hours after the rampage, police searched stores for shoppers and employees who were awaiting rescue.

A storage manager, her husband and three others hid in a storage room for about 40 minutes.

Three women in an antiques shop hid under a staircase until it was safe to leave.

Case #44. A store employee huddled in the corner of the men's clothing department with about a dozen other employees until police yelled to get out of the store.

Another employee went with co-workers and customers into a back closet, coming out about a half-hour later when police shouted to come out with their hands up.

Case #46. Students holed up in their dorm rooms and apartments, some staying until well after the university said the crisis was over.[438]

Case #59. Teacher Laura Feinstein hid with the children for about 40 minutes before law enforcement came for them.

Mass Shootings

E
S
C
Assess All Alternatives
P
E

- OFFENDER
- VICTIM
- ENVIRONMENT

Although it may seem almost impossible, if you are exposed to a mass shooting situation it is critical to *try to remain calm and keep your wits about you* in order to properly assess the situation. A knowledgeable decision about when and how to move or isolate yourself from the situation may mean the difference between life and death. The following section presents a methodology to properly assess the situation and determine one's next move.

A simple model for assessing a situation is the Crime Triangle. This model is commonly used in law enforcement for analyzing problem solving situations, and is a tool that could be applicable in mass shooting situations.

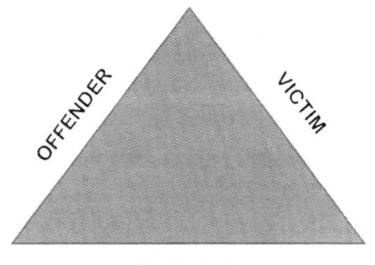

ENVIRONMENT

The Crime Triangle consists of three primary elements:
- **Offender** (the person who commits the crime);
- **Victim** (someone who is hurt by the actions of the offender), and
- **Location** (the incident environment, the place where the crime occurs)

During a critical incident such as a mass shooting, it is important to stay calm, to refrain from panic, and to analyze the three components of the Crime Triangle to the best of one's ability in order to make an informed decision.

For example: if you determine that the offender has not seen you and is moving away from your location, you may want to stay perfectly still until the offender has left the area. When safe to do so, you may be able to exit the building, removing yourself from harm or finding a better position of cover or concealment. Learning this step in the model is extremely important, as one must be able to quickly make some informed decisions before taking action.

Let's examine how by quickly assessing each side of the triangle we can make a more informed decision regarding our next moves during an active shooter situation.

The Crime Triangle: Offender

The first side of the triangle is the **offender**. What observations can you make about the offender which might help you to make a better decision as to the specific actions you are going to take?

One of the foremost observations is knowing what type of weapon or weapons the offender has at his disposal: does he have a handgun, shotgun or rifle? Does he have semi-automatic weapons or assault rifles? Information on the offender's weapons may provide an insight into how to respond. For example, a handgun is not nearly as accurate as a shotgun or rifle, especially at long distances (over 50 yards), and a shotgun usually has a smaller ammunition capacity than a rifle. This information may be extremely important when trying to decide if you should run and to where you should run.

Another important observation to make involves the demeanor and actions of the offender. Does he seem to be intent, almost on a mission and seeking specific targets, or just randomly shooting into a crowd?

Is the shooter aiming deliberately at a specific target?

If his actions appear to be cold and calculated as if he is seeking specific targets, you may decide to stay in a concealed position until he leaves the area. However, if he is frantic in nature and wildly spraying bullets everywhere, jumping behind the nearest cover may be the best option.

If you are in a safe place, you may want to observe the offender's clothing and his direction of movement in order to relay important information to responding officers. However, remember not to give up your position of safety and security to make observations. Also remember that just because an offender leaves the building or the area does not mean the incident is over or that he will not return to continue his rampage. If you are in a safe location, stay hidden until rescued by police.

Mass Shootings

The Crime Triangle: Victim

On this side of the triangle we will look at the characteristics of victim, which includes you as a participant in the event.

Are you safe and secure in your current position, or do you need to move to find cover or concealment? Are you injured? If so, are you incapacitated? A twisted ankle may give you pain but still allow you to exit, where a gunshot wound may keep you confined to your current location. Do you need life-saving attention? If necessary, can you move to a safer location? Answers to each one of these questions may dictate your next move.

Can you assist in protecting others, such as by barricading doors or escaping out windows? If you can help protect others without exposing yourself to danger, you may want to do so. The important caveat here is *without exposing yourself to danger*. <u>Your first duty is to remain safe at all times</u>. If you are killed or injured you are simply adding to the problem. This basic principle seems like common sense, yet even trained law enforcement officers must continually be reminded about officer safety.

Are you a caretaker for others such as small children or elderly adults? If so, you will want to focus on keeping them calm, reassuring them that everything will be OK, and working to keep them as safe as possible through the use of movement, cover or concealment. If you are a caretaker for others, this will have a significant impact on your decisions including when to move, where to move, and how to get there. If a member of your party is injured, especially critically, this also will factor into your assessment of the situation and ultimately your decision to take action.

If you can safety treat the injured, remember to continue to be aware of your surroundings at all times. Mass shootings are dynamic situations that can change in an instant. If you are knowledgeable regarding basic first aid, utilize those techniques on the most critical of injuries. In most situations you will not have access to even the most basic of first aid supplies, so be creative in identifying items to use: paper towels, napkins, even feminine hygiene products can be used to stop blood loss, and rolled-up newspapers tied with belts or shoestrings can serve as makeshift splints.

Finally, if you have a cell phone, determine whether you can quietly call or text your location to first responders so that when the incident is concluded they can locate severely injured parties in the most expeditious manner.

The Crime Triangle: Location/Environment

On this third side of the triangle, we examine the environment where these violent incidents occur. Environment certainly has played a significant role in many of the major shootings in this country. Using the Crime Triangle, we can quickly assess a situation and make appropriate decisions.

When assessing the environment, look around. Are you close to an exit or escape route, including doors or windows? Can you access a fire escape, stairwell or ladder? Can you run to safety via a hallway, or move strategically across an open area, going from object to object to provide concealment or cover?

Are you in a position that provides cover from gunfire or concealment from the offender's line of sight? Can you barricade or lock doors to protect yourself from the offender?

If not on the ground floor: can you escape out of a window or use something in the room to rappel out of the window if necessary? Are there trees to climb out onto, or bushes below that may break your fall? Can you lower yourself by hanging onto a window ledge and reducing the distance of the fall?

Though we have looked here at three separate aspects of the Crime Triangle, remember that this assessment should take only seconds. Prior time spent in assessing your surroundings, escape routes, exits, cover, or concealment will expedite this process in the event of a crisis.

Mass Shootings

E
S
C
A
PRESENT A SMALL TARGET
E

- **STAY LOW**
- **CRAWL OR RUN IN A CROUCHED POSITION**

Whether you are behind cover, concealing yourself from the shooter, or deciding to flee, **try to make yourself a small target**. Make it as difficult for the shooter as possible to get off a clean shot that could seriously wound or incapacitate you.

While hiding, roll up into a ball or get into the fetal position. Try to make yourself as small a target as possible by secreting yourself in locations where it would be difficult for the shooter to see you. If you are outside, a gutter, drainage ditch or even a large curb may provide adequate cover. If you are in a school or workplace, cabinets or closets may provide a place to curl up into a ball and say hidden from an offender. Other places to "get small" may include behind heavy furniture or under certain types of tables.

The key to presenting a small target is to quickly find a place where you can hide yourself and remain patient. Don't curl up into a ball out of the view of the offender and then as soon as you stop hearing gunfire peer out, exposing your head or other portions of your body. Remember that the shooter could be reloading or simply reacquiring targets. In some situations, the offender may go outside to reload or obtain more weapons before returning and continuing on his homicidal spree.

Don't assume too soon that it's safe to emerge from hiding

If you decide to exit the location by running, you can still present a small and much more difficult-to-hit target by running in a crouched position or hunched down. If possible and the conditions are right, you may want to present a small target by crawling from one location to another. Many moviegoers in the Aurora theater shooting presented a small target by crawling in between the rows of seats before finally deciding to exit out the nearest door.

Remember try not to call attention to yourself or draw the attention of the shooter. Running in short bursts while seeking cover or concealment may be safer then sprinting across an open area. Some research indicates that short sprints of two to three seconds don't allow an average shooter enough time to sight in on a moving target.

- **STAY LOW**
- **CRAWL OR RUN IN A CROUCHED POSITION**

Case #46. Desiree Smith said, "I dropped to the ground under my seat...everyone was army-crawling toward the back of the auditorium on the floor. As soon as I reached the door, I got halfway hunched over, and then started to run as soon as I got outside."

Case #56. Jennifer Seeger dove into the aisle and tucked herself under a chair, and Holmes shot the person behind her. "I just laid in a ball and waited for him to go..."

Mass Shootings

E
S
C
A
P
ENGAGE

The final step in the Six Steps to Survival Model is ENGAGE. Engaging or fighting the armed offender should occur **only as a last resort.**

- **ENGAGE ONLY AS A LAST RESORT**
- **ENGAGE WITH MULTIPLE INDIVIDUALS IF POSSIBLE**

Research indicates that when a single individual engages an armed offender, the individual almost always loses. From Luigi's restaurant to Ft. Hood, Texas to Virginia Tech, people with good intentions were killed engaging the shooter. That is why **attempting to fight back should be the last resort.**

Always keep in mind: **SAFETY FIRST.** If you are not safe, you cannot possibly help others. This is a mantra that police trainers have told their recruits for years. It's one that even casual travelers hear each time they board a plane and the flight attendants remind passengers that "in case of an emergency place the oxygen mask over your own face before attempting to assist others."

It is heroic to want to help and stop the violence, but research clearly indicates that in nearly every documented case, the shooter has the upper hand.

There are probably numerous reasons for this result, but the most common conjecture is that an unarmed, untrained, and strategically unprepared person simply cannot overcome a well-armed homicidal maniac who is intent on killing. Mentally, the bad guy is at the location to kill, while the individual is usually just the wrong person in the wrong place at the wrong time and ill-prepared mentally, physically or emotionally to take down a sociopathic murderer.

If fighting is one's only option, then a coordinated attack by multiple individuals overwhelming the offender is much more successful. The offender only has so many weapons and can get off only so many shots before succumbing to multiple punches, kicks, stabs or other types of offensive attacks by the potential victims.

Even more successful are when the attacks coincide with the offender's preoccupation with other tasks such as reloading his weapon. This was the case in Springfield, Oregon with school shooter Kip Kinkel, and with shooter Colin Ferguson on the Long Island Railroad train. In each case, the murderer was stopped while reloading his weapon, and attacked by multiple individuals.

- **ENGAGE ONLY AS A LAST RESORT**

Case #1. When Red McDaniel saw that his wife had been shot, he turned toward the shooter and charged him, placing him in a bear hug. He drove King out of the church even while taking shots to the chest. McDaniel died outside the church.

Kenneth Lee Truitt also went after the shooter. A witness said that when he got to the door he leaped into the air toward King, who was just outside the door. King shot him.[439]

Case #4. Restaurant manager Neva Caine got out of her booth and went to confront the man. Huberty shot once at point-blank range and Caine died within minutes.

Case #35. Stagehand Erin Halk and security guard Jeff Thompson rushed him {the killer} from opposite sides. Thompson was shot twice in the body and once in the leg; Halk was shot in the chest, hand and leg. Both were killed.

Case #42. Matthew Joseph LaPorte, an Air Force ROTC student, was reported to have attempted to tackle Seung-Hui Cho from behind but was fatally injured in the attempt.

Case #49. Captain John Gaffaney attempted to stop Hasan, either by charging the shooter or throwing a chair at him, but was mortally wounded in the process.

Witnesses reported that civilian physician assistant Michael Cahill tried to charge Hasan with a chair before being shot and killed.

Case #53. Randy Fannin confronted the gunman, saying "Please don't do this. There's another way. Let's go outside and talk." Fannin was shot and killed.

Case #55. Gloria Leonidas {was} in a parking lot when she was confronted by Stawicki. She and the gunman were arguing, and she knocked the gun from his hand before he fatally shot her in the head and stole her car.

- **ENGAGE ALONG WITH MULTIPLE INDIVIDUALS IF POSSIBLE**

Case #16. While {Ferguson was} reloading his third magazine, somebody yelled, "Grab him!" Three passengers tackled him and pinned him to one of the train's seats. Other passengers ran to grab his arms and legs and help hold him down.

Case #26. Student wrestler Jake Ryker tackled Kip Kinkel as he was attempting to reload his weapon. Several others quickly piled on and helped t hold the gunman until police arrived.

Case #51. As Jared Loughner stopped to reload he dropped the loaded magazine from his pocket to the sidewalk, and bystander Patricia Maisch grabbed it. Another bystander hit Loughner in the back of the head with a folding chair. The gunman was then tackled to the ground by 74-year-old retired U.S. Army Colonel Bill Badger, aided by others.

Mass Shootings

Summary

In examining the actions taken by individuals involved in mass shooting events over the past 30 years, it is possible to identify some tactics successfully utilized by survivors. Understanding that each situation is both unique in its circumstances and dynamic in its development, it is still possible to see that there are reccurring patterns of behavior that can provide insight into our response to these tragic events.

In examining the commonalities in the response of individuals over the past few decades, this research has provided a significant body of knowledge beyond the traditional *run, hide and fight* response. Individuals who fled the scene without drawing attention to themselves, or who found cover from the hostile fire, often lived to tell their tales of survival. Others who locked or barricaded doors and found creative places to hide throughout the event frequently survived the attacks.

Unfortunately, there have been more than enough mass shootings to identify trends and make suggestions on the actions one might take if ever confronted with a mass shooting incident. The intent of this book was to examine actions and identify activities which might increase a person's chances for survival if faced with one of these horrific events.

If there is any way possible to exit, seek cover or conceal yourself as opposed to engaging the offender: do so. Fighting back—especially if you are alone—is almost never a good idea, and should be used only as a last resort.

Mass Shootings

APPENDIX

<u>Mass shooting Case Studies in chronological order</u>

1. First Baptist Church, Daingerfield, Texas
   June 22, 1980

2. Bob Moore's Welding & Machine Shop, Miami, Florida
   August 20, 1982

3. Ianni's Nightclub, Dallas, Texas
   June 29, 1984

4. McDonald's Restaurant, San Ysidro, California
   July 18, 1984

5. U.S. Postal Service, Edmond, Oklahoma
   August 20, 1986

6. Shopping Center, Palm Bay, Florida
   April 23, 1987

7. Electromagnetic Systems Lab, Sunnyvale, California
   February 16, 1988

8. Cleveland Elementary School, Stockton, California
   January 17, 1989

9. Standard Gravure Printing Co., Louisville, Kentucky
   September 14, 1989

10. General Motors Acceptance Corp., Jacksonville, Florida
    June 18, 1990

11. Luby's Cafeteria, Killeen, Texas
    October 16, 1991

12. University of Iowa, Iowa City, Iowa
    November 1, 1991

Mass Shootings

13. Lindhurst High School, Olivehurst, California
    May 1, 1992

14. Office Building, San Francisco, California
    July 1, 1993

15. Luigi's Restaurant, Fayetteville, North Carolina
    August 6, 1993

16. Long Island Railroad, New York, New York
    December 7, 1993

17. Chuck E. Cheese Restaurant, Aurora, Colorado
    December 14, 1993

18. Fairchild Air Force Base, Spokane County, Washington
    June 21, 1994

19. Walter Rossler Co. Office, Corpus Christi, Texas
    April 3, 1995

20. Freddie's Fashion Mart, New York, New York
    December 8, 1995

21. Municipal Office, Fort Lauderdale, Florida
    February 9, 1996

22. R. E. Phelon Co. Plant, Aiken, South Carolina
    September 15, 1997

23. Caltrans Maintenance Yard, Orange, California
    December 19, 1997

24. Connecticut State Lottery Office, Newington, Connecticut
    March 6, 1998

25. Westside Middle School, Jonesboro, Arkansas
    March 24, 1998

26. Thurston High School, Springfield, Oregon
    May 21, 1998

Mass Shootings

27. Columbine High School, Littleton, Colorado
    April 29, 1999

28. Day Trading Firms, Atlanta, Georgia
    July 29, 1999

29. Wedgwood Baptist Church, Fort Worth, Texas
    September 15, 1999

30. Xerox Corp., Honolulu, Hawaii
    November 2, 1999

31. Radisson Bay Harbor Hotel, Tampa, Florida
    December 30, 1999

32. Edgewater Technology, Wakefield, Massachusetts
    December 26, 2000

33. Navistar International Engine Plant, DuPage County, Illinois
    February 5, 2001

34. Lockheed Martin Plant, Meridian, Mississippi
    July 8, 2003

35. Damageplan Concert, Columbus, Ohio
    December 8, 2004

36. Living Church of God, Brookfield, Wisconsin
    March 12, 2005

37. Red Lake High School, Red Lake, Minnesota
    March 21, 2005

38. Mail Processing Center, Goleta, California
    January 30, 2006

39. Rave After-party, Seattle, Washington
    March 25, 2006

Mass Shootings

40. Nickel Mines Amish School, Bart Township, Pennsylvania
    October 2, 2006

41. Trolley Square Mall, Salt Lake City, Utah
    February 12, 2007

42. Virginia Tech University, Blacksburg, Virginia
    April 16, 2007

43. Apartment Building, Crandon, Wisconsin
    October 7, 2007

44. Westroads Mall, Omaha, Nebraska
    December 5, 2007

45. City Council Meeting, Kirkwood, Missouri
    February 7, 2008

46. Northern Illinois Univesity, DeKalb, Illinois
    February 14, 2008

47. Pinelake Health & Rehab Center, Carthage, North Carolina
    March 29, 2009

48. American Civic Association Center, Binghamton, New York
    April 3, 2009

49. Fort Hood Army Base, Fort Hood, Texas
    November 5, 2009

50. Hartford Beer Distributorship, Manchester, Connecticut
    August 3, 2010

51. Rep. Gabrielle Giffords Public Meeting, Tucson, Arizona
    January 8, 2011

52. IHOP Restaurant, Carson City, Nevada
    September 6, 2011

53. Salon Meritage, Seal Beach, California
    October 12, 2011

Mass Shootings

54. Oikos University, Oakland, California
    April 2, 2012

55. Café Racer, Seattle, Washington
    May 30, 2012

56. Cinemark Movie Theater, Aurora, Colorado
    July 20, 2012

57. Sikh Temple, Oak Creek, Wisconsin
    August 5, 2012

58. Accent Signage Systems, Inc., Minneapolis, Minnesota
    September 27, 2012

59. Sandy Hook Elementary School, Newtown, Connecticut
    December 14, 2012

Mass Shootings

End Notes

[1] Fredreka Schouten, Meghan Hoyer and Paul Overberg, "Mass shootings toll exceeds 900 in past seven years." USA Today, February 22, 2013. [http://www.usatoday.com/story/news/nation/2013/02/21/mass-shootings-domestic-violence-nra/1937041/]

[2] Heather Mallick, "Mass shootings becoming sadly common the U.S." The (Toronto) Star, September 01, 2012. http://www.thestar.com/news/world/2012/09/01/mallick_mass_shootings_becoming_sadly_common_in_the_us.html

[3] "The Devil and Church Violence." Safeatchurch.org. [http://www.safeatchurch.org/the-devil-and-church-violence.html]

[4] "Daingerfield Shooting." Cop&Cross.org. [www.copandcross.org/daingerfield-shooting.html]

[5] Luisa Yanez, "Two decades after Miami murder spree, man who stopped killer talks." The Miami Herald, October 26, 2003.

[6] "Carl Robert Brown." Wikipedia The Free Encyclopedia. 16 December 2012. [http://en.wikipedia.org/wiki/Carl_Robert_Brown]

[7] "Carl Robert Brown." Murderpedia The Encyclopedia of Murderers. [http://murderpedia.org/male.B/b/brown-carl-robert.htm]

[8] Luisa Yanez. "Two decades after Miami murder spree, man who stopped killer talks," Ibid.

[9] Gary M. Lavergne, Worse Than Death: The Dallas Nightclub Murders and the Texas Multiple Murder Law. University of North Texas Press, 2003. Online review, [books.google.com/books/about/worse_than_death.html?id=Hr3OBwP-IbUC]

[10] "Abdelkrim Belachheb." Murderpedia The Encyclopedia of Murderers. [http://murderpedia.org/male.B/b/belachheb.htm]

[11] Susana Hayward, The Associated Press. "Rejected for dance, man kills woman, 5 others in nightclub." Gainesville (Florida) Sun, June 30, 1984. [http://news.google.com/newspapers?nid=1320&dat=19840630&id=-3oRAAAAIBAJ&sjid=kukDAAAAIBAJ&pg=2317,4756045]

[12] "It's An Enigma. Patrons at Ianni's Bar." [www.jcs-group.com/enigma/ fascinating/patrons.html]

[13] Ibid.

[14] "James Oliver Huberty," biography. [http://www.imdb.com/name/nm1272041/bio.]

[15] "James Huberty," Murderpedia The Encyclopedia of Murderers. [http://www.murderpedia.org/male.H/h/huberty-james.htm]

[16] "Gunman Kills 20 In California." Bangor Daily News, July 19, 1984. [http://news.google.com/newspapers?nid=2457&dat=19840719&id=2wQ1AAAAIBAJ&sjid=F08KAAAAIBAJ&pg=3984,1331552]

[17] "James Oliver Huberty," biography, Ibid.

Mass Shootings

[18] Amanda Covarrubias, Ernest Sander, the Associated Press. "Haunted By The Massacre At Mcdonald's." The Seattle Times, July 17, 1994. [http://community.seattletimes.nwsource.com/archive/?date=19940717&slug=1920774]

[19] "James Huberty." Murderpedia, Ibid.

[20] Ibid.

[21] Amanda Covarrubias, et al. "Haunted by the Massacre at McDonald's," Ibid.

[22] "James Oliver Huberty," Murderpedia, Ibid.

[23] Mara Bovsun. "Mailman massacre: 14 die after Patrick Sherrill 'goes postal' in 1986 shootings." New York Daily News, August 15, 2010. [http://www.nydailynews.com/news/crime/mailman-massacre-14-die-patrick-sherrill-postal-1986-shootings-article-1.204101]

[24] Jacob V. Lamar, Jr. "Crazy Pat's Revenge." Time Magazine, June 24, 2001. [http://www.time.com/time/magazine/article/0,9171,144859,00.html]

[25] Ibid.

[26] Ibid.

[27] "Patrick Henry Sherrill." Murderpedia The Encyclopedia of Murderers. [http://murderpedia.org/male.S/s/sherrill-patrick-henry.htm]

[28] Ibid.

[29] Ibid.

[30] Ibid.

[31] Ibid.

[32] Ibid.

[33] Jacob V. Lamar, Jr. "Crazy Pat's Revenge." Time Magazine, Ibid.

[34] "Patrick Henry Sherrill." Murderpedia, Ibid.

[35] Ibid.

[36] Ibid.

[37] Ibid.

[38] "Anger Remains 20 Years After Cruse's Rampage," Life on the Row. April 23, 2007. [http://lifeontherow.proboards.com/index.cgi?board=ond&action=display&thread=188]

[39] "Wiliam Cruse, Florida Death Row Inmate." Crime/Punishment. About.com, [http://crime.about.com.od/deathrow/ig/Florida-Death-Row-Inmates/William-Cruse.htm]

[40] "Anger Remains 20 Years After Cruse's Rampage." Life on the Row, Ibid.

[41] Ibid.

[42] Howard Benedict, Associated Press. "6 killed, 13 injured by shopping center gunman." Kentucky New Era, April 24, 1987. [http://news.google.com/newspapers?nid=266&dat=19870424&id=DOcrAAAAIBAJ&sjid=lwUGAAAAIBAJ&pg=1106,6972388]

[43] John A. Torres. "Palm Bay Killer Far From Execution 20 Years Later." The (Florida) Ledger, April 30, 2007. [http://www.theledger.com/article/20070430/NEWS/704300348?p=3&tc=pg]

[44] John A. Torres. "20 years after Palm Bay massacre, killer still far from execution." The Florida Times Union, April 29, 2007. [http://jacksonville.com/apnews/stories/042907/D8OQ6Q5O1.shtml]

[45] "Supermarket Employees Tells Her Story." Associated Press, April 25, 1987. [http://www.apnewsarchive.com/1987/Supermarket-Employees-Tells-Her-Story/id-d950a475dcd5ee11a40b5abe57339080]

[46] Kenneth Ofgang. "S.C. Upholds Death Sentence in Mass Killing at Silicon Valley Firm." Los Angeles Metropolitan News-Enterprise, July 3, 2009. [http://www.metnews.com/articles/2009/farl070309.htm]

[47] Dan Morain and Mark A. Stein, "Unwanted Suitor's Fixation of Woman Led to Carnage." Los Angeles Times, February 18, 1988. [http://articles.latimes.com/1988-02-18/news/mn-43514_1_mr-farley-richard-farley-sunnyvale-public-safety-department]

[48] "People v. Farley, No. S024833, July 02, 2009." FindLaw. [http://caselaw.findlaw.com/ca-supreme-court/1295931.html]

[49] Ibid.

[50] "Richard Wade Farley." Murderpedia The Encyclopedia of Murderers. [http://www.murderpedia.org/male.F/f/farley-richard.htm]

[51] "People v. Farley," FindLaw.com, Ibid.

[52] "Slaughter in a School Yard." TIME Magazine, June 24, 2001. [http://www.time.com/time/magazine/article.0,9171,151105.00.html]

[53] The Associated Press. "Five Children Killed As Gunman Attacks A California School." The New York Times, January 18, 1989. [http://www.nytimes.com/1989/01/18/us-five-children-killed-as-gunman-attacks-a-california-school.html]

[54] "Slaughter in a School Yard." TIME Magazine, Ibid.

[55] Nelson Kempsky, Chief Deputy Attorney General, and others. "A Report to Attorney General John K. Van de Kamp on Patrick Edward Purdy and the Cleveland School Killings." October 1989. Retrieved online at http://www.schoolshooters.info/PL/Subject-Purdy_files/Purdy%20-%20official%20report.pdf

[56] "Five Childred Killed as Gunman Attacks a California School." The New York Times, Ibid.

[57] The Associated Press. "Worker on Disability Leave Kills 7, Then Himself, in Printing Plant." The New York Times, September 15, 1989. [http://www.nytimes.com/1989/09/15/us/worker-on-disability-leave-kills-7-then-himself-in-printing-plant.html]

[58] "Joseph Thomas Wesbecker." Murderpedia, The Encyclopedia of Murderers. [http://murderpedia.org/male.W/w/wesbecker-joseph.htm]

[59] "Worker on Disability Leave Kills 7, Then Himself, in Printing Plant." The New York Times, Ibid.

[60] "James Edward Pough." Murderpedia The Encyclopedia of Murderers. [http://murderpedia.org/male.P/p/pough-james-edward.htm]

[61] Ron Word, Associated Press. "Official Puzzled Over Pough." The Gainsville Sun, June 24, 1990, p. 38. [http://news.google.com/newspapers?id=FPMRAAAAIBAJ&sjid=PuoDAAAAIBAJ&pg=6051,8213818&dq=pough]

[62] "James Edward Pough." Murderpedia, Ibid.

[63] Ibid.

[64] Ron Word, Associated Press. "Massacre memories remain." The Prescott (Arizona) Courier, June 17, 1991, page 7A.

[65] Ike Flores, Associated Press. "Silent gunman kills 10 people, himself in two days." Mohave Dailey Miner, June 19, 1990, p. 12. [http://news.google.com/newspapers?id=hD8LAAAAIBAJ&sjid=EVMDAAAAIBAJ&pg=6956,5985544&dq=pough]

[66] "Collections Darkest Day – GMAC Massacre 1990." CU Collector, June 18, 1990. [http://blog.cucollector.com/hot-topics/collections-darkest-day-%E2%80%93-gmac-massacre-1990/]

[67] "James Edward Pough: GMAC Massacre." Murder by City. Crime Library, Criminal Minds & Methods. [http://www.trutv.com/library/crime/photogallery/murder-by-city.html?corPhoto=12]

[68] Paula Chin, "A Texas Massacre." People Magazine, November 4, 1991. Vol. 36, No. 17. [www.people.com/people/archive/article/0,,20111193,00.html]

[69] Ibid.

[70] Terri Langford. "Massacre Survivor Haunted by Dreams with PM-Massacre Anniversary." AP News Archive. October 15, 1992. [http://www.apnewsarchive.com/1992/Massacre-Survivor-Haunted-by-Dreams-With-PM-Massacre-Anniversary/id-0ed7faf3fe10bff02eb9a0d941adc3c4]

[71] "George Jo Hennard." Murderpedia The Encyclopedia of Murderers. [http://murderpedia.org/male.H/h/hennard-george-jo.htm]

[72] Paula Chin. "A Texas Massacre," Ibid.

[73] "George Jo Hennard." Murderpedia, Ibid.

[74] Terri Langford, Associated Press. "Man dodges massacre in dishwasher." Ocala Star-Banner, October 18, 1991. [http://news.google.com/newspapers?nid=1356&dat=19911018&id=-igxAAAAIBAJ&sjid=QQcEAAAAIBAJ&pg=2695,5940001]

[75] "George Jo Hennard." Murderpedia, Ibid.

[76] Ibid.

[77] "Gang Lu." Murderpedia The Encyclopedia of Murderers. [http://murderpedia.org/male.L/l/lu-gang.htm]

[78] Steven Lee Myers. "Student Opens Fire at U. of Iowa, Killing 4 Before Shooting Himself." The New York Times, November 2, 1991. [http://www.nytimes.com/1991/11/02/us/student-opens-fire-at-u-of-iowa-killing-4-before-shooting-himself.html]

[79] Chris Earl. "University of Iowa Shootings: 20 Years Later." KCRG News, Nov. 1, 2011. [www.KCRG.com/news/local/University-of-Iowa-Shootings-20-Years-Later-132997028.html]

[80] "Gang Lu." Murderpedia, Ibid.

[81] Ibid.

[82] Ashley Gebb. "Supreme Court upholds Lindhurst shooter's death sentence." appealdemocrat.com, August 2, 2012. [http://www.appeal-democrat.com/articles/court-118322-death-school.html]

[83] "Eric Christopher Houston." Murderpedia The Encyclopedia of Murderers. [http://murderpedia.org/male.H/h/houston-eric.htm]

[84] Robert B. Gunnison, Ken Hoover, et al. "School Gunman Surrenders – 4 Killed in 10-Hour Ordeal," The San Francisco Chronicle, May 2, 1992. [Retrieved from http://mylifeofcrime.wordpress.com/2007/05/01/lindhurst-high-school-massacre/]

[85] "Eric Christopher Houston." Murderpedia, Ibid.

[86] Ibid.

[87] "Lindhurst high school shooting." Wikipedia The Free Encyclopedia. [en.wikipedia.org/wiki/Lindhurst_High_School_shooting]

[88] "The Hostage Taking of Lindhurst High School Classroom C106, May 1, 1992, as told by Johnny Mills." [http://www.columbine-angels.com/lindhurst_story.htm]

[89] Robert B. Gunnison, Ken Hoover, et al. "School Gunman Surrenders – 4 Killed in 10-Hour Ordeal." The San Francisco Chronicle, Ibid.

[90] "Gian Luigi Ferri." Murderpedia The Encyclopedia of Murderers. [http://murderpedia.org/male.F/f/ferri-gian-luigi.htm]

[91] "Victims of Chance in Deadly Rampage." The New York Times, July 7, 1993. [http://www.nytimes.com/1993/07/07/us/victims-of-chance-in-deadly-rampage.html]

[92] Jenifer Warren, Patt Morrison. "Roving Gunman Kills 8, Self in S.F. High-Rise." Los Angeles Times, July 2, 1993. [http://articles.latimes.com/1993-07-02/news/mn-9236_1_law-firm]

[93] "Gian Luigi Ferri." Murderpedia, Ibid.

[94] "Case 2: Kenneth Junior French." Death Penalty Curriculum. [http://deathpenaltycurriculum.org/student/c/courtroom/casestudies/case2-French.htm]

[95] "Kenneth Junior French." Murderpedia The Encyclopedia of Murderers. [http://murderpedia.org/male.F/f/french-kenneth-junior.htm]

[96] "(Sgt.) Kenneth Jr. French." Murderer's Profiles, Licensed to Kill. [www.deepfocusproductions.com/licensed_to_kill_profiles.php]

[97] "Case 2: Kenneth Junior French." Death Penalty Curriculum, Ibid.

[98] Ibid.

[99] Ibid.

[100] "Colin Ferguson." Murderpedia The Encyclopedia of Murderers. [http://murderpedia.org/male.F/f/ferguson-colin.htm]

[101] "Colin Ferguson." Crime/Punishment. about.com. [crime.about.com/od/murder/p/frguson.htm]

[102] "Colin Ferguson (mass murderer)." Wikipedia The Free Encyclopedia. Retrieved January 14, 2013. [en.wikipedia.org/wiki/Colin_Ferguson_%28mass_murderer%29]

[103] Ibid.

[104] Ibid.

[105] Frances X. Clines. "Death on the L.I.R.R.: The Rampage, Gunman in a Train Aisle Passes Out Death." The New York Times, Dec. 9, 1993. [http://www.nytimes.com/1993/12/09/nyregion/death-on-the-lirr-the-rampage-gunman-in-a-train-aisle-passes-out-death.html?src=pm]

[106] "Colin Ferguson." Murderpedia, Ibid.

[107] Ibid.

[108] Scott Kersgaard and Susan Greene. "Nathan Dunlap Death Row Case: Appeals Exhausted For Colorado Chuck E. Cheese's Killer," The Colorado Independent as reported on HuffPost Denver. February 20, 2013. [http://www.huffingtonpost.com/2013/02/20/nathan-dunlap-death-row-c_n_2724716.html]

[109] "Gunman Kills 4 Workers at Colorado Restaurant." The New York Times, December 16, 1993. [www.nytimes.com/1993/12/16/us/gunman-kills-4-workers-at-colorado-restaurant.html]

[110] Patrick Doyle, Natasha Gardner. "The Politics of Killing." The Denver Magazine, December 2008. [http://www.5280.com/magazine/2008/12/politics-killing]

[111] Ibid.

[112] "Gunman Kills 4 Workers at Colorado Restaurant." The New York Times, Ibid.

Mass Shootings

[113] Patrick Doyle, Natasha Gardner. "The Politics of Killing." The Denver Magazine, Ibid.

[114] "An Airman's Revenge: 5 Minutes of Terror." The New York Times, June 22, 1984. [www.nytimes.com/1994/06/22/us/an-airman-s-revenge-5-minutes-of-terror.html]

[115] "Dean A. Mellberg." Murderpedia The Encyclopedia of Murderers. [http://murderpedia.org/male.M/m/mellberg-dean.htm]

[116] "An Airman's Revenge: 5 Minutes of Terror." The New York Times, Ibid.

[117] "Dean A. Mellberg." Murderpedia, Ibid.

[118] Dan Parker. "Victims' families see season of renewal." Corpus Christi Caller-Times, April 3, 2000. [http://web.caller.com/2000/april/03/today/local_ne/4127.html]

[119] "James Daniel Simpson." Murderpedia, The Encyclopedia of Murderers. [http://murderpedia.org/male.S/s/simpson-james-daniel.htm]

[120] "Dan Parker, Victims' families see season of renewal." Corpus Christi Caller-Times, Ibid.

[121] Ibid.

[122] Hy Drusin, "Massacre at Freddy's in Harlem: Fire Fueled by Anti-Semitism Kills 8." Jewish Post. [www.jewishpost.com/archives/news/massacre-at-freddy's-in-harlem-fire-fueled-by-anti-semitism-kills-8.html]

[123] John Kifner, "8 Killed in Harlem – Arson/Gunman among dead." San Francisco Chronicle, December 9, 1995.[www.sfgate.com/news/article/PAGE-ONE-8-Killed-in-Harlem-Arson-Gunman-3018812.php]

[124] Ibid.

[125] Hy Drusin. "Massacre at Freddy's in Harlem: Fire Fueled by Anti-Semitism Kills 8." Jewish Post, Ibid.

[126] Freida Ratliff Frisaro, Associated Press. "Ex-worker Kills 5, Self." February 10, 1996. The Free Library. [http://www.thefreelibrary.com/EX-WORKER+KILLS+5%2c+SELF%5cFired+Florida+parks+employee+vowed+revenge.-a083904308]

[127] The Miami Herald. "Disgruntled ex-employee kills five, self." The Ocala (Florida) Star-Banner, February 10, 1996. [http://news.google.com/newspapers?nid=1356&dat=19960210&id=mzwxAAAAIBAJ&sjid=ewcEAAAAIBAJ&pg=5487,3983060]

[128] Freida Ratliff Frisaro. Associated Press, "Ex-worker Kills 5, Self," Ibid.

[129] "Clifton McCree." Murderpedia The Encyclopedia of Murderers. [http://murderpedia.org/male.M/m/mccree-clifton.htm]

[130] "Hastings Arthur Wise." [www.clarkprosecutor.org/html/death/US/wise992.htm]

[131] Jeffrey Collings, Associated Press. "Man who killed 4 in Aiken County plant put to death." The State.com, reprinted in Murderpedia.org. [http://murderpedia.org/male.W/w1/wise-hastings.htm]

[132] Associated Press. "Factory shooter's path to execution nears end." The Augusta Chronicle, October 30, 2005. [http://old.chronicle.augusta.com/ stories/2005/10/30/met_17717.shtml]

Mass Shootings

[133] Associated Press. "S.C. plant shooter is facing execution." (Wilmington, North Carolina) Star-News, October 30, 2005. [http://news.google.com/newspapers?nid=1454&dat=20051030&id=jw9PAAAAIBAJ&sjid=nx8EAAAAIBAJ&pg=6732,4242016]

[134] "Hastings Arthur Wise." clarkprosecutor.org, Ibid.

[135] "Hastings Arthur Wise." Murderpedia The Encyclopedia of Murderers. [http://murderpedia.org/male.W/w1/wise-hastings-photos.htm]

[136] South Carolina Bureau. "Workers describe slayings." The Augusta Chronicle, January 29, 2001. [http://chronicle.augusta.com/stories/2001/01/29/met_309358.shtml]

[137] South Carolina Bureau. "4 killed in Aiken County shooting; suspect caught by SWAT team." The Augusta Chronicle, September 16, 1997. [http://chronicle.augusta.com/stories/1997/09/16/met_214740.shtml]

[138] "Man who killed 4 in Aiken executed." Charleston (South Carolina) The Post and Courier, November 5, 2005. [http://news.google.com/newspapers?nid=2482&dat=20051105&id=oklJAAAAIBAJ&sjid=kgkNAAAAIBAJ&pg=1362,1491357]

[139] South Carolina Bureau. "Survivors go on; Wise waits for execution." The Augusta Chronicle, November 4, 2005. [http://chronicle.augusta.com/stories/2005/11/04/met_19187.shtml]

[140] Nick Anderson, Lee Romney, David Haldane. "Aftermath of Killer's Fury." Los Angeles Times, December 20, 1997. [http://articles.latimes.com/1997/dec/20/news/mn-431]

[141] Ibid.

[142] Nick Anderson, et al. "Aftermath of Killer's Fury." Los Angeles Times, Ibid.

[143] Nick Anderson, David Reyes, and Esther Schrader. "4 Workers, Gunman Die in Caltrans Yard Attack." Los Angeles Times, December 19, 1997. [http://articles.latimes.com/1997/dec/19/news/mn-172]

[144] Ibid.

[145] Jonathan Rabinovitz. "Rampage in Connecticut: The Overview; Connecticut Lottery Worker Kills 4 Bosses, Then Himself." The New York Times, March 07, 1998. [http://www.nytimes.com/1998/03/07/nyregion/rampage-connecticut-overview-connecticut-lottery-worker-kills-4-bosses-then.html?pagewanted=all&src=pm]

[146] Strat Douthat. "Conn. Lottery Worker Kills 4, Self." AP News Archive. March 7, 1998. [http://www.apnewsarchive.com/1998/Conn-Lottery-Worker-Kills-4-Self/id-ecf2612d0abe7f48227d8bfd9d39036f]

[147] Associated Press. "Lottery Victim Begged For His Life." CBS News. February 11, 2009. [http://www.cbsnews.com/2100-201_162-4442.html]

[148] Jonathan Rabinovitz. "Rampage in Connecticut: the Overview," The New York Times, Ibid.

[149] "Five die in Connecticut rampage." Lubbock (Texas) Avalanche-Journal, March 7, 1998. [http://lubbockonline.com/stories/030798/LA0694.shtml]

[150] Ibid.

[151] Associated Press. "Lottery Victim Begged for His Life." CBS News, Ibid.

[152] "Five die in Connecticut rampage." Lubbock (Texas) Avalanche-Journal, Ibid.

[153] Mass Shooting Incidents in America (1984-2012) – Westside Middle School. [http://www.nycrimecommission.org/initiative1-shootings.php]

[154] "Mitchell Scott Johnson." Murderpedia The Encyclopedia of Murderers. [http://www.murderpedia.org/male.J/j/johnson-mitchell.htm]

[155] "Andrew Douglas Golden." Murderpedia The Encyclopedia of Murderers. [http://murderpedia.org/male.G/g/golden-andrew.htm]

[156] Julie Deardorff. "4 Pupils, Teacher Die In Schoolyard Ambush." Chicago Tribune, March 25, 1998. [http://articles.chicagotribune.com/1998-03-25/news/9803250187_1_pupils-teacher-school-grounds]

[157] Jenny Price. "Heroes Emerge From Ark. Shooting." AP News Archive. Mar. 26, 1998. [http://www.apnewsarchive.com/1998/Heroes-Emerge-From-Ark-Shooting/id-32b67db4efd8b17266988f58450ae469]

[158] Ibid.

[159] "Andrew Douglas Golden." Murderpedia, Ibid.

[160] "Kipland P. Kinkel." Murderpedia The Encyclopedia of Murderers. [http://murderpedia.org/male.K/k/kinkel-kipland.htm]

[161] Ibid.

[162] Jeff Barnard, Associated Press. "One Dies in Jeff School Shooting." (Alabama) Times Daily, May 21, 1998. [http://news.google.com/newspapers?nid=1842&dat=19980521&id=TEseAAAAIBAJ&sjid=L8cEAAAAIBAJ&pg=1422,3411743]

[163] "Kip Kinkel." Wikipedia, The Free Encyclopedia. [en.wikipedia.org/wiki/Kip_Kinkel]

[164] Associated Press. "One Slain, 5 Critical At Oregon High School - Police Find Two More Dead At Home Of Shooter, 15." The Seattle Times, May 21, 1998. [http://community.seattletimes.nwsource.com/archive/?date=19980521&slug=2751975]

[165] Jeff Barnard. "One Dies in School Shooting," (Alabama) Times Daily, Ibid.

[166] "Columbine High School massacre." Wikipedia, The Free Encyclopedia. February 3, 2013. [en.wikipedia.org/wiki/Columbine_High_School_massacre]

[167] Ibid.

[168] Ibid.

[169] Ibid.

[170] Ibid.

[171] Ibid.

Mass Shootings

[172] " Injured and Survivors of the Columbine High School Shooting." [http://www.acolumbinesite.com/victim/injured.html]

[173] Dave Cullen. Columbine (Book). Scribd. April 6, 2009. [http://www.scribd.com/doc/100886158/Columbine-Book]

[174] Associated Press. "Columbine massacre survivors push ahead." NBC News, April 20, 2009. [http://www.nbcnews.com/id/30294427/#.UTVAr1eH-So]

[175] "The Columbine High School Shootings." The Criminal Mind. [http://vanessawest.tripod.com/columbine-4.html]

[176] Victor Medina. "Columbine High's armed guard saved student lives." Examiner.com, December 24, 2012. [http://www.examiner.com/article/fact-check-columbine-high-s-armed-guard-saved-student-lives]

[177] Dave Cullen. Columbine, Ibid.

[178] Victor Medina. "Columbine High's armed guard saved student lives." Examiner.com, Ibid.

[179] Dave Cullen. Columbine, Ibid.

[180] Ibid.

[181] "Columbine High School massacre." Wikipedia, The Free Encyclopedia. February 3, 2013. [en.wikipedia.org/wiki/Columbine_High_School_massacre]

[182] "The Columbine High School Shootings." The Criminal Mind, Ibid.

[183] Dave Cullen. Columbine, Ibid.

[184] Ibid.

[185] Ibid.

[186] Ibid.

[187] Victor Medina. "Columbine High's armed guard saved student lives,"Examiner.com, Ibid.

[188] Mark Orrin Barton." Murderpedia The Encyclopedia of Murderers. [http://murderpedia.org/male.B/b/barton-mark.htm]

[189] "Portrait of a killer. Time Magazine, August 9, 1999. [http://www.time.com/time/magazine/article/0,9171,991676,00.html]

[190] "Note from killer hints at revenge." CNN, July 30, 1999. [http://articles.cnn.com/1999-07-30/us/9907_30_atlanta.shooting.07_1_note-death-toll-pain/3?_s=PM:US]

[191] Associated Press. "Disgruntled investor, sought in killing of 12, kills self." AP Archive, July 30, 1999. [https://docs.google.com/document/d/10KNth8BgKhLheRyqBd_SBg38XZMdp4bv7rRbkKzJZxA/edit?hl=en_US]

[192] "Mark Orrin Barton." Murderpedia, Ibid.

[193] Ibid.

[194] "Larry Gene Ashbrook." Murderpedia The Encyclopedia of Murderers. [http://murderpedia.org/male.A/a/ashbrook-larry.htm]

[195] Ibid.

[196] "Church shooter leaves few clues as to why he went on rampage." Lubbock (Texas) Avalanche-Journal, September 17, 1999. [http://lubbockonline.com/stories/091799/sta_0917990087.shtml]

[197] Ibid.

[198] Ibid.

[199] Jim Yardley. "Gunman Opens Fire at a Texas Church; Kills 7 and Himself." The New York Times, September 16, 1999. [http://partners.nytimes.com/library/national/091699texas-shoot.html]

[200] Katherine Ramsland. "Psychiatry, the Law, and Depravity: Profile of Michael Welner, M.D. Chairman, The Forensic Panel." Crimelibrary – Criminal Minds and Methods. [http://www.trutv.com/library/crime/criminal_mind/forensics/welner/5.html]

[201] Byran Koji Uyesugi." Murderpedia The Encyclopedia of Murders. [http://murderpedia.org/male.U/u/uyesugi-byran.htm]

[202] Ibid.

[203] Ronen Zilberman. Associated Press. "Survivors emerge as key witnesses." (Honolulu) Star Bulletin, May 16, 2000. [http://archives.starbulletin.com/2000/05/16/news/story1.html]

[204] Ibid.

[205] Steve Huettel, Linda Gibson, Kathryn Wexler. "Gunman kills 5." St. Petersburg Times, December 31, 1999. [http://www.sptimes.com/News/123199/TampaBay/Gunman_kills_5.shtml]

[206] "Ibid.

[207] David Pedreira, Graham Brink. "Motive for targeting co-workers still unknown." St. Petersburg Times, December 31, 1999. [http://www.sptimes.com/News/123199/TampaBay/Motive_for_targeting_.shtml]

[208] Mike Clary. "5 Killed, 3 Hurt in Florida Hotel Shooting." Los Angeles Times, December 31, 1999. [http://articles.latimes.com/1999/dec/31/news/mn-49342]

[209] Huettel, Gibson, and Wexler. "Gunman kills 5," St. Petersburg Times, Ibid.

[210] Ibid.

[211] J.R. Ross, The Associated Press. "Tampa Gunman Kills 5 .Radisson Bay Harbor Employee Opens Fire in Hotel Full of New Year's Tourists." The Ledger, Lakeland, Florida, December 31, 1999. [http://news.google.com/newspapers?nid=1346&dat=19991231&id=iMtOAAAAIBAJ&sjid=Y_0DAAAAIBAJ&pg=5304,6458176]

[212] Ibid.

[213] Ibid.

[214] "Michael McDermott." Murderpedia The Encyclopedia of Murderers. [http://murderpedia.org/male.M/m/mcdermott-michael.htm]

[215] Nadya Labi. "Portrait Of A Killer." Time Magazine, December 31, 2000. [http://www.time.com/time/magazine/article/0,9171,93313,00.html]

[216] Ibid.

[217] Greg Sukiennik, Associated Press. "Officials: Rampage may have been triggered by IRS dispute." Lubbock Avalanche-Journal, December 27, 2000. [http://lubbockonline.com/stories/122700/upd_075-5889.shtml]

[218] Pam Belluck. "Ex-Worker Opens Fire at Illinois Plant; 5 Are Killed." The New York Times, February 6, 2001. [http://www.nytimes.com/2001/02/06/us/ex-worker-opens-fire-at-illinois-plant-5-are-killed.html]

[219] Alex Rodriguez, Matt O'Connor. "Navistar Gunman Got Past Cracks In Gun Law." Chicago Tribune, February 7, 2001.

[220] Tammy Webber, Associated Press. "Five dead in shooting at Illinois plant." Lubbock Avalanche-Journal, February 5, 2001. [http://lubbockonline.com/stories/020501/upd_075-7284.shtml]

[221] "5 Dead, 8 Wounded in Shooting Rampage." WDAM, July 8, 2003. [http://www.wdam.com/story/1352618/5-dead-8-wounded-in-shooting-rampage]

[222] Matt Volz, Associated Press. "Gunman opens fire at Lockheed Martin plant in Mississippi; six dead including shooter." The Florida Times-Union, July 8, 2003. [http://jacksonville.com/tu-online/apnews/stories/070803/D7S5HSKO0.html]

[223] "5 Dead, 8 Wounded in Shooting Rampage." WDAM, Ibid.

[224] Ibid.

[225] DAMAGEPLAN Shooting: What Happened The Night DIMEBAG Was Murdered?" Dimebag Darrell Tribute, December 8, 2004. Originally published in The Columbus Dispatch, Janury 16, 2005. [http://www.dimebagdarrelltribute.com/what_happened_the_night_dimebag_died.html]

[226] "Nathan Miles Gale." Murderpedia The Encyclopedia of Murderers. [http://murderpedia.org/male.G/g/gale-nathan.htm]

[227] Ibid.

[228] Ibid.

[229] "DAMAGEPLAN Shooting: What Happened The Night DIMEBAG Was Murdered?" Dimebag Darrell Tribute, Ibid.

[230] Ibid.

[231] "Three Years After DIMEBAG's Murder: Missed Opportunities Abound." December 8, 2007. [http://www.blabbermouth.net/news.aspx?mode=Article&newsitemID=86362]

[232] "Nathan Miles Gale." Murderpedia, Ibid..

[233] "Dimebag Darrell." Wikipedia, the free encyclopedia. January 10, 2013. [en.wikipedia.org/wiki/Dimebag_Darrell]

[234] "Terry Ratzmann." Wikipedia The Free Encyclopedia. February 18, 2013. [http://en.wikipedia.org/wiki/Terry_Ratzmann]

[235] "Terry Michael Ratzmann." Murderpedia The Encyclopedia of Murderers. [http://murderpedia.org/male.R/r/ratzmann-terry.htm]

[236] Ibid.

[237] Associated Press. "Gunman's job on line before rampage." Lubbock Avalanche-Journal, March 14, 2005. [http://lubbockonline.com/stories/031405/nat_031405011.shtml]

[238] Ibid.

[239] Associated Press. "Wounded Boy Reached Out to Minn. Shooter." FOX News. March 24, 2005. [http://www.foxnews.com/story/0,2933,151450,00.html]

[240] Joshua Freed, The Associated Press. "Teen who killed seven at high school believed to have acted alone." The Seattle Times, March 22, 2005. [http://seattletimes.com/html/nationworld/2002215403_shoot22.html]

[241] Kirk Johnson. "Survivors of High School Rampage Left With Injuries and Questions." The New York Times, March 25, 2005. [http://www.nytimes.com/2005/03/25/national/25shoot.html?_r=0]

[242] "Jeffrey James Weise." Murderpedia The Encyclopedia of Murderers. [http://murderpedia.org/male.W/w/weise-jeffrey.htm]

[243] Ibid.

[244] "Teen who killed 9 claimed Nazi leanings." NBC News, March 23, 2005. [http://www.nbcnews.com/id/7259823/print/1/displaymode/1098]

[245] "Jeffrey James Weise." Murderpedia, Ibid.

[246] Joshua Freed. "Teen who killed seven at high school believed to have acted alone." The Seattle Times, Ibid.

[247] "Jeffrey James Weise." Murderpedia, Ibid.

[248] Kirk Johnson. "Survivors of High School Rampage Left With Injuries and Questions." The New York Times, Ibid.

[249] "Postal killer acted irrational years before attack." NBC News. February 1, 2006. [http://www.nbcnews.com/id/11128315/#.UTY4q1eH-So]

[250] Katherine Ramsland. "Female Mass Murderers: Major Cases and Motives." crimelibrary. [http://www.trutv.com/library/crime/notorious_murders/mass/female_mass_murderer/1.html]

[251] Ibid.

[252] "Jennifer San Marco." Murderpedia The Encyclopedia of Murderers. [http://murderpedia.org/female.S/s/san-marco-jennifer.htm]

Mass Shootings

[253] Tim Molloy, Associated Press. "Shooter In Postal Rampage Had Psychological Problems." The (Owasso, Michigan) Argus-Press, February 1, 2006. [http://news.google.com/newspapers?nid=1988&dat=20060201&id=eHkiAAAAIBAJ&sjid=GK0FAAAAIBAJ&pg=1331,2622008]

[254] "Postal killer acted irrational years before attack." NBC News, Ibid.

[255] Associated Press. "Mayhem Stalks The Early-Morning Dregs Of An All-Night Party." KOMO News, Apr 1, 2006. [http://www.komonews.com/news/archive/4181536.html]

[256] "Kyle Aaron Huff." Murderpedia The Encyclopedia of Murderers. [http://murderpedia.org/male.H/h/huff-kyle.htm]

[257] "Mayhem Stalks The Early-Morning Dregs Of an All-Night Party." KOMO News, Ibid.

[258] Seattle Times via Associated Press. "Gunman kills six, self in Seattle home." USA Today, March 26, 2006. [http://usatoday30.usatoday.com/news/nation/2006-03-25-seattle-shooting_x.htm]

[259] Ibid.

[260] "Kyle Aaron Huff." Murderpedia, Ibid.

[261] "Mayhem Stalks The Early-Morning Dregs Of An All-Night Party." KOMO News, Ibid.

[262] Ibid.

[263] Ibid.

[264] "Kyle Aaron Huff." Murderpedia, Ibid.

[265] "Mayhem Stalks The Early-Morning Dregs Of An All-Night Party." KOMO News, Ibid.

[266] "Amish school shooting." Wikipedia The Free Encyclopedia. January 25, 2013. [en.wikipedia.org/wiki/Amish_school_shooting]

[267] Associated Press. "5th girl dies after Amish schoolhouse shooting." [http://www.nbcnews.com/id/15105305/ns/us_news-crime_and_courts/t/th-girl-dies-after-amish-schoolhouse-shooting/]

[268] "Lancaster Co. School Shooting Leaves Four Dead." KYW.com, Oct. 2, 2006. [http://web.archive.org/web/20061002205912/http://cbs3.com/topstories/local_story_275115123.html]

[269] "5th girl dies after Amish schoolhouse shooting," Ibid.

[270] "Amish school shooting." Wikipedia, Ibid.

[271] Ibid.

[272] Chris Francescani. "'Shoot Me First,' Amish Girl Said to Ask." ABC News, Oct. 5, 2006. [http://abcnews.go.com/TheLaw/story?id=2531138&page=1]

[273] "Little Known About Utah Mall Killer." CBS News, February 11, 2009. [http://www.cbsnews.com/2100-201_162-2473373.html]

[274] Ibid.

[275] Ibid.

Mass Shootings

[276] Associated Press. "Off-Duty Officer Prevented Massacre in Salt Lake City Mall Shooting Spree, Police Say." FOX News, February 14, 2007. [http://www.foxnews.com/story/0,2933,251864,00.html]

[277] "Sulejman Talovic." Murderpedia The Encyclopedia of Murderers. [http://murderpedia.org/male.T/t/talovic-sulejman.htm]

[278] Jennifer Dobner, The Associated Press. "Police: Teen Shot Mall Victims at Random." The Washington Post, February 13, 2007. [http://www.washingtonpost.com/wp-dyn/content/article/2007/02/13/AR2007021300105.html]

[279] "Off-Duty Officer Prevented Massacre in Salt Lake City Mall Shooting Spree, Police Say." FOX News, Ibid.

[280] "Gunman Kills Five People at Trolley Square." (Utah) KSL.com, February 13, 2007. [http://www.ksl.com/?nid=148&sid=888784]

[281] Associated Press. "Gunman Kills 5 in Shooting Spree at Salt Lake City Mall Before Being Killed by Police." FOX News, February 13, 2007. [http://www.foxnews.com/story/0,2933,251603,00.html]

[282] "Little Known About Utah Mall Killer," CBS News.

[283] "Seung-Hui Cho." Wikipedia The Free Encyclopedia. February 19, 2013. [en.wikipedia.org/wiki/Seung-Hui_Cho]

[284] Ibid.

[285] "Worst U.S. shooting ever kills 33 on Va. campus," msnbc.com and NBC News, updated 4/17/2007. [http://www.nbcnews.com/id/18134671/ns/us_news-crime_and_courts/t/worst-us-shooting]

[286] Kevin Caruso. "What Happened: The Virginia Tech Massacre." Virginia Tech Massacre.com. [http://www.virginiatechmassacre.com/what-happened-virginia-tech-massacre.html]

[287] "Worst U.S. shooting ever kills 33 on Va. campus," msnbc.com and NBC News.

[288] "Kevin Granata." Wikipedia The Free Encyclopedia. [en.wikipedia.org/wiki/Kevin_Granata]

[289] "Seung-Hui Cho." Murderpedia The Encyclopedia of Murderers. [http://murderpedia.org/male.C/c/cho-seung-hui.htm]

[290] "Virginia Tech massacre timeline." Wikipedia The Free Encyclopedia. [en.wikipedia.org/wiki/Virginia_Tech_massacre_timeline]

[291] "Liviu Librescu." Wikipedia The Free Encyclopedia. [en.wikipedia.org/wiki/Liviu_Librescu]

[292] "Virginia Tech massacre." Wikipedia The Free Encyclopedia. [en.wikipedia.org/wiki/Virginia_Tech_massacre]

[293] "Seung-Hui Cho." Murderpedia, Ibid.

[294] "Virginia Tech massacre." Wikipedia, Ibid.

[295] Ibid.

Mass Shootings

[296] "Kevin Granata." Wikipedia, Ibid.

[297] Kate McGinty. "Horror and healing in Crandon-Killings tear at fabric of tight-knit community." (Wisconsin) Post-Crescent, October 14, 2007. [http://www.postcrescent.com/article/99999999/APC0101/710140525/Horror-healing-Crandon]

[298] "Tyler James Peterson." Murderpedia The Encyclopedia of Murderers. [http://murderpedia.org/male.P/p/peterson-tyler.htm]

[299] Raquel Rutledge. "Shooter sought refuge with friend's family." (Milwaukee) Journal Sentinel, Oct. 9, 2007. [http://www.jsonline.com/news/wisconsin/29291139.html]

[300] "People You'll See in Hell: Tyler Peterson." [http://pysih.com/2007/10/07/tyler-peterson/]

[301] "Nebraska Mall Shooter Broke Up With Girlfriend, Lost Job Before Massacre." FoxNews.com, December 06, 2007. [http://www.foxnews.com/story/0,2933,315441,00.html]

[302] "Police: Nine killed in shooting at Omaha mall, including gunman." CNN, December 6, 2007. [http://www.cnn.com/2007/US/12/05/mall.shooting/]

[303] "Nebraska Mall Shooter Broke Up With Girlfriend, Lost Job Before Massacre," FoxNews.com, Ibid.

[304] "Police: Nine killed in shooting at Omaha mall, including gunman," CNN, Ibid.

[305] Ibid.

[306] Kate Taylor. "I-Reporter recalls horror of Nebraska mall shootings." CNN, December 5, 2007. [http://articles.cnn.com/2007-12-05/us/mall.shooting.irpt_1_westroads-mall-von-maur-jewelry-store?_s=PM:US]

[307] "Omaha Gunman's Note: "Now I'll Be Famous"." CBS News, February 11, 2009. [http://www.cbsnews.com/8301-201_162-3582740.html]

[308] "Gunman Kills Eight, Then Himself, at Omaha Shopping Mall." Fox News, December 6, 2007. [http://www.foxnews.com/story/0,2933,315342,00.html]

[309] "Charles Lee Thornton." Murderpedia The Encyclopedia of Murderers. [http://murderpedia.org/male.T/t/thornton-charles.htm]

[310] Ibid.

[311] Ibid.

[312] Ibid.

[313] Ibid.

[314] The Chicago Tribune. "Police: There were no red flags." Sun Sentinel, February 16, 2008. [http://articles.sun-sentinel.com/2008-02-16/news/0802150299_1_gunman-medication-stephen-p-kazmierczak]

[315] Abbie Boudreau and Scott Zamost. "CNN Excusive: Secret files reveal NIU killer's past." CNN.com/crime. [http://www.cnn.com/2009/CRIME/02/13/niu.shooting.investigation/]

[316] "Stephen Phillip Kazmierczak." Murderpedia The Encyclopedia of Murderers. [http://murderpedia.org/male.K/k/kazmierczak.htm]

[317] U.S. Fire Administration/Technical Report Series: Northern Illinois University Shooting." USFA-TR-167/February 2008. [http://www.usfa.fema.gov/downloads/pdf/publications/tr_167.pdf]

[318] Chicago Tribune reporters. "Northern Illinois University shooting leaves 6 dead, 16 wounded." Los Angeles Times, February 14, 2008. [http://www.latimes.com/news/nationworld/nation/la-na-shooting15feb15,0,3655394.story]

[319] Josh Noel, James Kimberly, Robert Mitchum. "'I was prepared for that to be my last moment'--Attacker fired wordlessly into a mass of students." Chicago Tribune, February 15, 2008. [http://articles.chicagotribune.com/2008-02-15/news/0802150151_1_gunfire-junior-shoot]

[320] Ibid.

[321] Chicago Tribune Reporters. "Northern Illinois University shooting leaves 6 dead, 16 wounded." Los Angeles Times, Ibid.

[322] Josh Noel et al. "I was prepared for that to be my last moment." Chicago Tribune, Ibid.

[323] Ibid.

[324] Robert Mitchum, Chicago Tribune. "Student: 'All I saw was the flash of shooting'." Los Angeles Times, February 14, 2008. [http://www.latimes.com/news/nationworld/nation/la-na-eyewitness15feb15,0,882237.story]

[325] Chicago Tribune Reporters. "Northern Illinois University shooting leaves 6 dead, 16 wounded." Los Angeles Times, Ibid.

[326] Ibid.

[327] Ibid.

[328] Associated Press. "Police: Gunman's wife worked at care home." NBC News, March 30, 2009. [http://www.nbcnews.com/id/29944382/#.UTZTiVeH-So]

[329] "Carthage nursing home shooting." Wikipedia The Free Encyclopedia. [en.wikipedia.org/wiki/Carthage_nursing_home_shooting]

[330] Ibid.

[331] "Police: Gunman's wife worked at care home." NBC News, Ibid.

[332] "Robert Kenneth Stewart." Murderpedia The Encyclopedia of Murderers. [http://murderpedia.org/male.S/s/stewart-robert-kenneth.htm]

[333] Shaila Dewan. "Alleged Gunman's Wife Worked at Nursing Home." The New York Times, March 30, 2009.
[http://www.nytimes.com/2009/03/31/us/31shooting.html?_r=0]

[334] Michael Zennie. "Robert Stewart guilty of 2nd-degree murder, sentenced to life in prison." The Fayetteville (North Carolina) Observer, Sep. 04, 2011.
[http://www.fayobserver.com/articles/2011/09/03/1120314?sac=Home]

[335] "Binghamton struggles to understand why gunman killed 13." CNN, April 5, 2009.
[http://www.cnn.com/2009/CRIME/04/04/binghamton.shooting/index.html]

[336] Joe Kemp, Mathew Lysiak, Corky Siemaszko. "Who is Jiverly Voong aka Jiverly Wong?" New York Daily News, April 4, 2009. [www.nydailynews.com/news/jiverly-voong-aka-jiverly-wong-conflicting-picture-binghamton-gunman-emerges-article-1.359248?]

[337] "Binghamton shootings." Wikipedia The Free Encyclopedia. February 3, 2013.
[en.wikipedia.org/wiki/Binghamton_shootings]

[338] "Jiverly Antares Wong." Murderpedia The Encyclopedia of Murderers.
[http://murderpedia.org/male.W/w/wong-jiverly.htm]

[339] Ibid.

[340] Ibid.

[341] "Binghamton struggles to understand why gunman killed 13." CNN, Ibid.

[342] Joe Kemp, Matthew Lysiak. "Survivor of Binghamton massacre tried in vain to save his wife." NY Daily News. April 6, 2009. [http://www.nydailynews.com/news/survivor-binghamton-massacre-vain-save-wife-article-1.360199]

[343] Mike Baker and Brett Blackledge. "Ft. Hood UPDATES: New Clues in Military Base Shooting." Huff Post, 11/06/09.[http://www.huffingtonpost.com/2009/11/06/ft-hood-updates-new-clues_n_348157.html]

[344] Nidal Malik Hasan." Murderpedia The Encyclopedia of Murderers.
[http://murderpedia.org/male.H/h/hasan-nidal.htm]

[345] Jeremy Schwartz. "Witnesses in Fort Hood shooting hearing say Hasan returned to shoot same victims over and over." (Austin) Statesman.com, Oct. 15, 2010.
[http://www.statesman.com/news/news/state-regional/witnesses-in-fort-hood-shooting-hearing-say-hasan-/nRykN/]

[346] "Nidal Malik Hasan." Murderpedia, Ibid..

[347] Brad Knickerbocker, "Alleged Fort Hood shooter Maj. Nidal Hasan faces March 2012 trial." The Christian Science Monitor, July 20, 2011.
[http://www.csmonitor.com/USA/Military/2011/0720/Alleged-Fort-Hood-shooter-Maj.-Nidal-Hasan-faces-March-2012-trial]

[348] Jay Root. "Officer Describes Firefight That Downed Hasan." NBC DFW, Nov 7, 2009.
[http://www.nbcdfw.com/news/local/Officer-Describes-Firefight-That-Downed-Hasan-69488762.html]

[349] "Nidal Malik Hasan." Murderpedia, Ibid.

[350] Charley Keyes. "Despite alarming detail, Fort Hood shooting case still mysterious." CNN. November 17, 2010.
[http://www.cnn.com/2010/CRIME/11/17/texas.fort.hood.case/index.html]

[351] Charley Keyes. "Witnesses recount bloody scenes at Fort Hood hearing." CNN. October 20, 2010.
[http://www.cnn.com/2010/CRIME/10/19/texas.fort.hood.shootings/index.html]

[352] "Omar S. Thornton." Murderpedia The Encyclopedia of Murderers.
[http://murderpedia.org/male.T/t/thornton-omar.htm]

[353] Ray Rivera and Liz Robbins, "Troubles Preceded Connecticut Workplace Killing." The New York Times, August 3, 2010.
[http://www.nytimes.com/2010/08/04/nyregion/04shooting.html?pagewanted=all]

[354] "Jared Lee Loughner." Murderpedia The Encyclopedia of Murderers.
[http://murderpedia.org/male.L/l/loughner-jared.htm]

[355] Ibid.

[356] "Giffords Gunman Jared Loughner Jailed For Life," Sky News, November 9, 2012.
[http://news.sky.com/story/1008950/giffords-gunman-jared-loughner-jailed-for-life]

[357] "2011 Tucson shooting." Wikipedia The Free Encyclopedia. February 15, 2013.
[en.wikipedia.org/wiki/2011_Tucson_shooting]

[358] "Jared Lee Loughner." Murderpedia, Ibid.

[359] "2011 Tucson shooting." Wikipedia, Ibid.

[360] "Eduardo Sencion." Murderpedia The Encyclopedia of Murderers.
[http://murderpedia.org/male.S/s/sencion-eduardo.htm]

[361] "IHOP shooting death toll rises to 5." CBS News, September 7, 2011.
[http://www.cbsnews.com/2100-201_162-20102475-2.html]

[362] Steve Keegan. "Four dead, nine wounded in Nevada shooting." Barrie (Ontario) Examiner, September 6, 2011. [http://www.thebarrieexaminer.com/2011/09/06/four-dead-nine-wounded-in-nevada-shooting-5]

[363] "Accused Seal Beach Killer subdued with pepper balls in jail." Los Angeles Times, January 20, 2013. [http://latimesblogs.latimes.com/lanow/2013/01/accused-seal-beach-salon-killer.html]

[364] Paul Bentley, David Gardner, Mark Duell. "'He lived for his son': Gunman 'shot dead eight in beauty salon massacre to get back at hairdresser wife over custody battle'." The (U.K.) Daily Mail. October 13, 2011. [http://www.dailymail.co.uk/news/article-2048470/Seal-Beach-shooting-8-killed-Scott-Dekraai-targets-ex-wife-Orange-county-hair-salon.html]

[365] "DA seeks death penalty in salon murders." Sun Newspapers, October 14, 2011.
[http://www.sunnews.org/latest-news/da-seeks-death-penalty-in-salon-murders/]

[366] Associated Press. "Some say Calif. gunman was ex-husband." CBSnews.com, October 13, 2011. [http://www.cbsnews.com/2100-201_162-20119641.html]

Mass Shootings

[367] "Scott Evans Dekraii." Murderpedia The Encyclopedia of Murderers. [http://murderpedia.org/male.D/d/dekraai-scott.htm]

[368] "8 killed in Southern California salon shooting." CNS News, October 12, 2011. [http://cnsnews.com/8-killed-southern-california-salon-shooting-2]

[369] "Some say Calif. gunman was ex-husband," CBSnews.com, Ibid.

[370] "Scott Evans Dekraii." Murderpedia, Ibid.

[371] Terry Collins, "One Goh, Oikos University Shooting Suspect, Deemed Unfit For Trial," (San Francisco) The Huffington Post, January 7, 2013. [http://www.huffingtonpost.com/2013/01/07/one-goh-oikos_n_2428444.html]

[372] Matthias Gafni et al. "Oakland university shooting: Accused Oilos University shooter One Goh was 'troubled,' 'angry,' said those who knew him. Oakland Tribune, April 3, 2012. [http://www.insidebayarea.com/oakland-tribune/ci_20314383/oakland-school-rampage-suspect-sought-revenge-against-administrator]

[373] David Gardner, Rob Cooper, Meghan Keneally. "Oakland massacre gunman's boasts about violence revealed as relatives mourn students shot 'because they didn't do what he said'." The Daily Mail, April 2, 2012. [http://www.dailymail.co.uk/news/article-2124173/Oakland-shooting-Gunman-One-Gohs-boasts-massacre-Oikos-University-California-revealed.html]

[374] Ibid.

[375] Gillian Mohney. "Oikos University Shooting: Suspect, One L. Goh, Detained; At Least 7 Dead." ABC News. April 2, 2012. [http://abcnews.go.com/US/oakland-shooting-dead-oikos-university-suspect-idd-goh/story?id=16056854]

[376] Ibid.

[377] Mary Slosson, Lalit K Jha. "Indian among the seven killed in Oakland shooting incident." DNA India, Apr 3, 2012. [http://www.dnaindia.com/world/report_indian-among-the-seven-killed-in-oakland-shooting-incident_1670789]

[378] Jim Vojtech, Alyssa Newcomb, and Michael S. James. "Seattle Café Shooter Kills 5, and Himself After Citywide Manhunt." ABC News, May 31, 2012. [http://abcnews.go.com/US/ian-stawicki-seattle-cafe-racer-shooter-kills-shoots-citywide/story?id=16463885&singlePage=true#.UVnlgRzvu8c]

[379] "Police laud 'hero' in Seattle shootings." Fox News, June 1, 2012. [http://www.foxnews.com/us/2012/06/01/police-laud-hero-in-seattle-shootings/]

[380] Ibid.

[381] "Police: 'Hero' saved several Seattle cafe patrons as gunman opened fire." CNN, May 31, 2012. [http://www.cnn.com/2012/05/31/us/washington-cafe-shooting]

[382] "Police laud 'hero' in Seattle shootings." Fox News, Ibid.

[383] Gene Johnson, Shannon Dininny, Associated Press. "Police laud 'hero' in Seattle shootings." Columbian.com, June 1, 2012. [http://www.columbian.com/news/2012/jun/01/police-laud-hero-seattle-shootings/?print]

[384] Casey Mcnerthney. "Police credit homeless felon for helping at tragic shooting." KOMO News, June 1, 2012. [http://www.komonews.com/news/local/Police-credit-homeless-felon-for-helping-at-tragic-shooting-156495735.html]

[385] "Seattle shootings: day of horror, grief in a shaken city." The Seattle Times, May 30, 2012. [http://seattletimes.com/html/localnews/2018316552_roosevelt31m.html]

[386] Trevor Hughes and Gary Strauss. "Death penalty sought for James Holmes, trial set for Feb. 2014." USA Today, April 2, 2013. [http://www.usatoday.com/story/news/nation/2013/04/01/holmes-court-appearance-today/2041881/]

[387] Michael Muskal. "Questions, but few answers, in Colorado shooting; 12 dead, dozens hurt." Los Angeles Times, July 20, 2012. [http://articles.latimes.com/2012/jul/20/nation/la-na-nn-colorado-shooting-update-batman-20120720]

[388] "2012 Aurora shooting." Wikipedia The Free Encyclopedia. February 24, 2013. [en.wikipedia.org/wiki/2012_Aurora_shooting]

[389] "Aurora Colorado Shooting Tragedy From a Local's Perspective." Empower Network, August 3, 2012. [http://www.empowernetwork.com/freedombacknow/blog/aurora-colorado-shooting-tradegy-from-a-local/]

[390] "2012 Aurora shooting." Wikipedia, Ibid.

[391] Ibid.

[392] Jennifer Brown. "12 shot dead, 58 wounded in Aurora movie theater during Batman premier." The Denver Post, July 21, 2012. [http://www.denverpost.com/news/ci_21124893/12-shot-dead-58-wounded-aurora-movie-theater]

[393] Ryan Parker, Joey Bunch, Kurtis Lee, John Ingold, Jordan Steffen, Jennifer Brown. "Family identifies 27-year-old victim of Aurora theater shooting." The Denver Post, July 20, 2012. [http://www.denverpost.com/breakingnews/ci_21118201/unknown-number-people-shot-at-aurora-movie-theater]

[394] Sari Horwitz, Debbi Wilgoren. "Police say Colorado shooting suspect James Holmes had 2 pistols, assault rifle, shotgun." The Washington Post, July 20, 2012. [http://failover.washingtonpost.com/world/national-security/colorado-shooter-identified-as-james-holmes-24/2012/07/20/gJQAWkdrxW_story_2.html]

[395] "Aurora witnesses describe shooter's entrance, chaos." CBS News, July 20, 2012. [http://www.cbsnews.com/8301-505263_162-57476424/aurora-witnesses-describe-shooters-entrance-chaos/]

[396] Ryan Parker et al. "Family identifies 27-year-old victim of Aurora theater shooting," The Denver Post, Ibid.

[397] Jennifer Brown. "12 shot dead, 58 wounded in Aurora movie theater during Batman premier." The Denver Post, Ibid.

[398] Miguel Bustillo, Shelly Banjo, Tamara Audi. "Theater Rampage Jolts Nation." The Wall Street Journal, July 21, 2012. [http://online.wsj.com/article/SB10000872396390444464304577538292604705890.html]

[399] Ed Pilkington, Matt Williams. "Colorado theater shooting: 12 shot dead during The Dark Knight Rises screening." The (U.K.) Guardian, July 20, 2012. [http://www.guardian.co.uk/world/2012/jul/20/colorado-theater-shooting-dark-knight]

[400] "Shooting at Sikh temple in Wisconsin leaves at least 7 dead, including gunman." Published August 6, 2012 on FoxNews.com. [http://www.foxnews.com/us/2012/08/05/possible-injuries-after-shooting-at-sikh-temple-in-wisconsin/]

[401] Brian Louis, Henry Goldman and Christ Christoff. "Wisconsin Sikh Shooting Suspect Formed Skinhead Bands." Bloomberg News, August 7, 2012. [http://www.bloomberg.com/news/print/2012-08-06/wisconsin-sikh-shooting-probed-by-fbi-as-domestic-terror.html]

[402] "Shooting at Sikh temple in Wisconsin leaves at least 7 dead, including gunman." FoxNews.com, Ibid.

[403] Ted Rowlands, CNN, "Sikhs repair, reclaim temple after rampage." CNN.com, August 10, 2012. [http://www.cnn.com/2012/08/09/justice/wisconsin-temple-shooting/index.html]

[404] Brian Louis, et al. "Wisconsin Sikh Shooting Suspect Formed Skinhead Bands." Bloomberg News, Ibid.

[405] Matt McKinney. "Accent Signage Systems shooting: First victims fought for their lives." (Minneapolis) Star Tribune, October 2, 2012. [http://www.startribune.com/loacl/minneapolis/html?refer=y]

[406] Jennifer Bjorhus and Todd Nelson. "Accent rebuilds after Minneapolis workplace rampage." (Minneapolis) Star Tribune, April 5, 2013.

[407] "Illegal Gun Crime - Mass Shooting Incidents in America (1984-2012), Sandy Hook Elementary School." Citizens Crime Commission of New York City. [http://www.nycrimecommission.org/initiative1-shootings.php]

[408] John Christoffersen. "Newtown Shooting Motive Remains Unclear Following Search Warrant Revelations On Adam Lanza." Huff Post CRIME, March 29, 2013. [http://www.huffingtonpost.com/2013/03/29/newtown-shooting-motive_n_2978093.html]

[409] M. Alex Johnson and Becky Bratu. "Police: Second person injured in Connecticut school shooting survived." NBCnews.com, December 17, 2012.

http://usnews.nbcnews.com/_news/2012/12/17/15969867-police-second-person-injured-in-connecticut-school-shooting-survived?lite

[410] "Sandy Hook Elementary School shooting." Wikipedia The Free Encyclopedia. February 24, 2013. [en.wikipedia.org/wiki/Sandy_Hook_Elementary_School_shooting]

[411] John Christoffersen. "Newtown Shooting Motive Remains Unclear." Huff Post CRIME, Ibid.

[412] Ibid.

[413] Ibid.

[414] Ibid.

[415] "New York Daily News 2012 Person of the Year winner: The brave faculty of Sandy Hook Elementary School." New York Daily News, December 30, 2012, updated December 31, 2012. [http://www.nydailynews.com/new-york/new-york-daily-news-2012-person-year-winner-brave-faculty-sandy-hook-elementary-school-article-1.1230018?pgno=2]

[416] Christine Roberts. "Teacher's words of comfort to class during Newtown rampage: 'I love you all very much ... it's going to be OK'." New York Daily News, December 18, 2012. [http://www.nydailynews.com/news/national/sandy-hook-teacher-speaks-ordeal-article-1.1222727]

[417] "Sandy Hook Elementary School shooting." Wikipedia, Ibid.

[418] Ibid.

[419] "Teacher died fighting for her students." The Houston Chronicle, December 15, 2012. [http://www.chron.com/news/nation-world/nation/article/Teacher-died-fighting-for-her-students-4121117.php]

[420] Eileen FitzGerald. "Principal, school psychologist ran to help." (Danbury, Connecticut) News Times, December 14, 2012. [http://www.newstimes.com/news/article/Principal-school-psychologist-ran-to-help-4119969.php]

[421] Lia Eustachewich. "Connecticut victims ID'd as police uncover 'very good evidence' of shooter's motives." New York Post, December 15, 2012. [http://www.nypost.com/p/news/local/connecticut_victims_shooter_motives_dM0QIY1PQjY7PxV1pebrJK]

[422] "Sandy Hook Elementary School shooting." Wikipedia, Ibid.

[423] Billy Nilles. "Sandy Hook Teacher Who Died Shielding Special Needs Boy, 6, Like 'Jesus'." Hollywood Life, December 20, 2012. [http://hollywoodlife.com/2012/12/20/sandy-hook-special-ed-teacher-funeral-anne-marie-murphy/]

[424] "Sandy Hook Elementary School shooting," Wikipedia, Ibid.

[425] "Sandy Hook Classroom Survivor Played Dead." ABC News, Dec 17, 2012. [http://abcnews.go.com/blogs/headlines/2012/12/sandy-hook-classroom-survivor-played-dead/]

[426] "Colin Ferguson (mass murderer)." Wikipedia, Ibid.

[427] "Blood stains Oregon high school." CNN, May 21, 1998. [http://www.cnn.com/US/9805/21/shooting.pm/index.html]

[428] See Note 205.

[429] See Note 219.

[430] See Note 239.

[431] See Note 302.

[432] See Note 319.

[433] Scott Weber. "8 Dead in Shooting at Seal Beach Hair Salon." NBC Los Angeles, October 13, 2011. [http://www.nbclosangeles.com/news/local/6-Killer-in-Shooting-at-Seal-Beach-131627203.html]

[434] See Note 393.

[435] Ibid.

[436] David Fahrenthold, Sari Horwitz, Bill Turque. "Gunman opens fire at Colorado movie theater, killing 12." The Washington Post, July 20, 2012. [http://www.washingtonpost.com/national/gunman-opens-fire-at-colorado-movie-theater-killing-12/2012/07/20/gJQA6l75yW_story_1.html]

[437] See Note 24.

[438] See Note 316.

[439] "Daingerfield Shooting." Cop&Cross.org. [www.copandcross.org/daingerfield-shooting.html]

John Matthews is Executive Director of the Community Safety Institute (CSI) and an Assistant Chief Deputy Constable for Dallas County Constable's Office Precinct #1. Chief Matthews has developed more than 100 law enforcement and public safety initiatives for government agencies including the Department of Justice (DOJ); Bureau of Justice Assistance (BJA); Office of Community Oriented Policing Services (COPS); Department of Homeland Security (DHS); Office of Domestic Programs (ODP); Department of the Interior (DOI); Bureau of Indian Affairs, Office of Justice Services (OJS); and the Department of Transportation (DOT).

Matthews has been in law enforcement for nearly 30 years and is a Master Peace Officer and certified law enforcement instructor. With bachelor's and master's degrees in Administrative Management and an Advanced Law Enforcement Certificate, he is nationally recognized for his work in law enforcement and school safety issues. While working with the Dallas Police Department he was named *Outstanding Law Enforcement Officer* and was awarded a Certificate of Commendation from the Texas State Senate. He also received numerous departmental awards including *Certificate of Merit, Life Saving Award, Certificate for Civic Achievement,* and the *Police Commendation.* John currently serves as Senior Advisor to the National Sheriffs' Association, and Special Advisor to the National Law Enforcement Officer's Memorial Fund.

John is an award-winning writer, photographer, and the author of five books including *The Eyeball Killer*, a true crime Book of the Month and firsthand account of his capture of Dallas' only serial killer; the story has been adapted for network television shows. His books *School Safety 101* and *Neighborhood Watch 101* focus on making our communities safer and more secure and have been the cornerstones of training programs for thousands of law enforcement officers, educators, and their community stakeholders. He has been keynote speaker at education and law enforcement conferences around the country.

John hosted a safety segment on FOX-4 television in north Texas, and for three years was a talk show host on KRLD/CBS radio and the Texas State Network, where he still makes guest appearances. His numerous media appearances include NBC Nightly News, FOX News Channel, Leeza, The O'Reilly Report, Good Morning New York, Good Morning Texas, Good Day Dallas, Law Enforcement Television Network, A Current Affair, and local ABC, CBS, FOX and NBC television and radio affiliates.

Mass Shootings

Mass Shootings

Community Safety Institute (CSI) is a public safety consulting organization providing curriculum development, program design and project management, organizational assessments, and training and technical assistance in the areas of law enforcement, school and university safety, and homeland security. For nearly two decades CSI has developed and delivered dozens of nationally-recognized law enforcement and public safety training programs for the Department of Justice (DOJ); Department of Homeland Security (DHS); Department of Defense (DOD); Department of Education (ED), and Department of the Interior (DOI), serving both as a direct grantee of and a contractor to the nation's largest public safety associations and law enforcement organizations. During that time CSI has trained thousands of law enforcement officers, educators, and citizens while assisting hundreds of law enforcement agencies in implementing initiatives to decrease crime and improve the quality of life in communities throughout our nation.

For the federal government and its public safety partners CSI has developed and delivered law enforcement initiatives including: *Law Enforcement and Mental Health Partnerships I* and *II*; the *STAR initiative*; *COPS Native American Training Series I, II,* and *III*; *Jail Information Model* for the Office of Community Oriented Policing Services (COPS); the *Neighborhood Watch Toolkit*, the *Schools and Universities Safety Resource Center* (SUSRC) (both presidential-directed initiatives); the *Native American Neighborhood Watch Best Practices*, *Advanced Human Trafficking*, *Pandemic Planning for Courts* and *Continuity of Operations Planning (COOP) for Sheriffs* for the Bureau of Justice Assistance (BJA); *Protecting Special Events* for the U.S. Attorney General's Office (USAG); *Law Enforcement Leadership Training* for the Bureau of Indian Affairs (BIA); Community Policing Assessments for the U.S. Parks Service, Department of Interior (DOI); *Safe School* program, *Youth Guns, Gangs and Drugs* program, *Managing Juvenile Operations* and *Native American Juvenile Justice* program for the Office of Juvenile Justice and Delinquency Prevention (OJJDP); and multiple *Weapons of Mass Destruction* programs for Department of Homeland Security (DHS) including *Jail Evacuation* I and II, *WMD and the Community*, and WMD executive level course *Managing the Incident*.

Partnering with the National Sheriffs' Association and funded by BIA, CSI developed the nationally renowned *Neighborhood Watch Toolkit* and training series. To date, over two dozen separate and distinct training curricula and accompanying materials have been developed for this series, and provided by CSI staff to hundreds of NW groups and thousands of volunteers across the country.

For the past four years CSI has partnered with the Upper Midwest Community Policing Institute and has been responsible for all development and delivery of the *Native American Training Series (NATS) I, II, II* and *IV*, provided to Native American and Alaska Native communities, and the development and dissemination of the *Human Trafficking in Indian Country* initiative. Our work in Indian country also includes the development of the *Native American Neighborhood Watch Best Practices*, and the Village Public Safety Officer distance learning series for the Alaska State Troopers. For the Bureau of Indian Affairs, Office of Justice Services, CSI developed and delivers their *Basic Law Enforcement Supervisory Training p*rogram, and the *Coaching and Mentoring for Supervisors* training.